GOD

the Universe and Where I Fit In

A PSYCHIC'S REFLECTIONS ON FIGURING OUT THE REST OF YOUR LIFE

LAURIE ANN LEVIN, Psy.D.

Health Communications, Inc.
Deerfield Beach, Florida

www.hcibooks.com

Library of Congress Cataloging-in-Publication Data

Levin, Laurie Ann, 1953-
   God, the universe, and where I fit in : a psychic's reflections on figuring out the
rest of your life / Laurie Ann Levin.
    p. cm.
  ISBN-13: 978-0-7573-1440-7
  ISBN-10: 0-7573-1440-6
   1. Levin, Laurie Ann, 1953-   2. Religious biography.   3. Psychics—
Biography.   I. Title.
  BF1997.L48A3 2009
  133.8092—dc22
  [B]

                                                    2009020552

Publisher: Health Communications, Inc.
           3201 S.W. 15th Street
           Deerfield Beach, FL 33442–8190

Cover design Larissa Hise Henoch
Interior design by Lawna Patterson Oldfield
Interior formatting by Dawn Von Strolley Grove

GOD

the Universe
and Where I Fit In

This book is dedicated to:

My mother, who in her life and in her death gave me dimensions and inspiration.

My father, who knew that love is all there is.

My children, Jessica and Aaron, I love you, and in loving you, I see God's face.

Elena, for always expressing her true nature.

Frances, whose tenacity and passion led us all here.

Kim, for the love and hope of knowing that we are always just where we need to be.

Jerry, "if the sandman brought me dreams of you—
I'd wanna sleep my whole life through."
—as sung by Frank Sinatra

CONTENTS

FOREWORD

WHEN WE ARE FACED WITH palpably perilous periods of fear and tumult, why don't most of us stop long enough to ask the only questions that matter: *Who am I and why am I here?* As I have finally discovered, that voice of godlike guidance is actually inside all of us, accompanied by a messenger of elevated consciousness sitting by our side. For me, fortunately, that messenger—that channel to the other side—is embodied in the electrified presence of my wife and partner, Dr. Laurie Ann Levin. I want to share her with you in the form of this searching memoir, in the exposition of her rarefied questioning, and in her striking intimacy with so many souls who have presumably passed.

Who am I, you ask, or rather who was I? I was a résumé poster child, a symbol of the empty trinity of success, power, and money. For a time, as the CEO of the world's largest media and entertainment company, Time Warner Inc., I cycled through the anxious uptick of overwrought praise into the insidious downbeat of hyperbolic criticism. I sorted my identity into three separate and unequal compartments: first and foremost work, family second, and third, a hidden compartment of caged rage and unexpressed arrogance. In the absence of a higher power, the universe was benignly indifferent for me. For most of my adult existence, I maintained my own impenetrable iron curtain, secluding my emotions from any visible contact.

All of that began to unravel when I was starkly awakened by the force of 9/11. In tears, I reviewed the lifelong passing of those I loved who had left me, or so I thought, one by one—starting with the untimely passing of my hauntingly autistic older sister and then my endearing, adoring grandma, followed by my earnestly driven father, and, pivotally, the unspeakable murder of my heroically gifted son, ending with the death of my sweet, but depressed mom.

At age sixty-three, I knew I was profoundly clueless. I had no solid conception of who I truly was, yet knew that I needed to change, to figure out the rest of my life.

Never did I dare dream that that resolution was on its way; that my salvation would be mediated by a remarkably beautiful and fun-loving woman. Laurie energetically presented me with a full-blown belief system of love and light, of trust, protection, and connection, of no-holds-barred openness tied to the purity of overtly naked emotions. She taught me how to listen to the soft voice that inspires us to pause, to take a beat, and to intuit the universal truth that material loss and loss of life are merely illusions.

As for the question *Why am I here?* the simple answer is to be of service, to be a healer, and to put my life's amazing experiences at the service of others.

What my wife, my spiritual initiator, has given me, I lovingly give to you, for I do know, at last, where I fit in!

—*Gerald M. Levin, Santa Monica, May 2009*

ACKNOWLEDGMENTS

WHEN I WAS IN SHOW BUSINESS, there were just a few single-owner agencies that succeeded. Roger Strull, with his soft-spoken gumption, left William Morris Agency and started his own TV literary agency, Preferred Artists. Ever so rarely a TV writer would write a "spec" screenplay. Roger sent me such a client's work. The writing was elegant, dramatic, funny, intelligent—a joy to read. There was detail in the construction and wordsmithing, and refinement in the description and dialogue. I called Roger to meet his writer. His name was Philip Jayson Lasker. His most recent credit was co-executive producer of *The Golden Girls*. I asked Roger if I could read everything available from Phil. Every couple of months, I was sent a new spec screenplay, each more inventive than the previous.

I don't know what I expected Phil to look like, but the first time I laid eyes on him he looked like a missing member of the Ramones: goatee, black garb, thick Forest Hills accent, slender and slight. He chain-smoked, drank coffee to excess, and yet somehow seemed calm. I loved his laugh. He'd swiftly turn a conversation into a platform for a few funny lines. Phil appreciated himself. That is so intoxicating . . . to be in the presence of someone who is enjoying themselves, but not to the exclusion of you. Of course, he was keenly aware of my level of enjoyment too, yet he was loving his wit, enjoying the laughter, repeating his joke, laughing again—it was a circle of excitement that I immediately wanted more of.

We worked on several projects together, until one was finally produced, entitled *Man from Elysian Fields*, starring Andy Garcia, Mick Jagger, James Coburn, Anjelica Huston, and Julianna Margulies. I took the naked, unencumbered spec screenplay to producers who found the money, the stars, and the director.

I had already set my next career as a doctor of psychology in motion, along with an early stage development of a holistic institute, and I followed my gut to not take a production credit.

Later, when I had five thousand pages of a book that I had written over the course of fifteen years, I asked my dear friend, Phil, one of the smartest, kindest men I know, to help. Phil lives in Maine with his equally talented, compassionate wife, Suzanna, and their animals in Jefferson with one gas station and a general store.

We worked, we three, for many months on end—romancing the five thousand pages to two hundred. If not for Phil and Suzanna, along with honored help from his deceased brother, Joel, we would all be sitting in a paper stew of ramblings and ravings.

Thank you both for the light, laughter, and lessons learned. Thank you both for the generosity of prose and pot roast. You took me in as family and gave me your hearts and minds. I acknowledge, respect, thank, and love you.

Please let me also acknowledge all the brilliance of HCI in order of appearance in my life: Gary, Peter, Tom, Allison, Michele, Larissa, Kim, and all the unknown many who help every day in so many ways.

Chapter One

Not Seeing Is Believing

Dreams are true while they last,
and do we not live in dreams?

LORD ALFRED TENNYSON

TENNYSON HAD A POINT. I spent most of my childhood alone, cavorting within the boundaries of my own imagination. The mind is not an unusual sandbox for a child to play in. Because both my mother and father drank and swallowed numerous colorful pills, I escaped more and more into the walled-up refuge of my silent thoughts.

My father, Stanley Perlman, was a huge bear of a man, six feet five inches, with hands as big as hams and a smile as bright and caressing as sunlight. I loved to climb up in his lap, put my

1

arms around his tree trunk of a neck, and settle into the warm pillow of his cheek. His bulk and personality could fill any room, leaving that room more than empty when he was gone.

He was gone a lot.

Before my father decided to attach our financial fate to the quixotic Florida real estate market, he was a traveling salesman, constantly on the road peddling his family's line of housecoat dresses. As dads often do, he would promise to someday take me on the road with him, but then he would leave before I woke without so much as saying good-bye.

I would stand in the living room for hours on end, staring out the window hoping to see his car coming around the corner. My mother, Germaine, or as she called herself, Gerry, too young and ill-equipped to handle two babies and long periods of self-sufficiency, would finally become exasperated with my forlorn face and send me to my room. Why was I punished for exhibiting honest emotion, I couldn't fathom. Looking back, I'm quite certain that she watched me in such a rattled state of longing for my father that she suffered the very human daggers of jealousy.

My mother was nothing if not extremely human.

With the pressures piling on her shoulders over the years, my mother housed herself inside a brick exterior. In the eyes of a child, she was powerful and unrelenting, much like an armored tank. I took her deportment at face value, which, as we all come to learn as we grow older, has little to do with true value.

If anything, a tough outer shell is usually a sure sign that the soul inside is drowning in a whirlpool of pain and self-doubt. At a very tender age I figured out that what you see is half of what you get. In sharp contrast to my own emotional personality, I do remember that my mother allowed herself the luxury of tears one time, when her own mother died.

Most children who find themselves alone in that same situation would quickly conjure up an imaginary friend. Someone who, though invisible, would love them, understand them, and, best of all, never leave them suddenly for business trips out of town. Why I never bothered to whip up an imaginary friend I don't know. In retrospect, it would have been nice to have someone under the same roof that was always on my side. However, my root personality made that impossible. It always seemed that the apple dangling from the highest limb of the tallest tree is what I found the most tantalizing.

As I look back on it now, I feel that the core reason why I didn't fantasize about an invisible friend is because I felt so terribly invisible myself. Rather than play jacks in my room with a best friend who didn't exist, I spent those lonely hours believing that I was put on this earth with a mission: I was a messenger of God.

I'm more than a little embarrassed to admit that I don't remember exactly what that message was; I do know that I refused to write it down for fear someone else may find it and then that person would become the messenger of God. Nevertheless, I do remember how believing that I was handpicked for this all-important task down here on Earth made me feel blessedly important. If only in the backstreets of my own imagination, I was a somebody.

When I was very young, my mother made me say my prayers before going to bed. "Now I lay me down to sleep, I pray the Lord my soul to keep. If I should die before I wake, I pray the Lord my soul to take." It's questionable whether any prayer with the word "die" in it should be the last thing on a child's lips before nodding off, but I don't remember feeling any shiver of panic as I snuggled my small frame beneath the thick covers. In fact, the opposite proved to be true. Long after my mother kissed me on the forehead and turned out the light, I would remain awake, and in my childlike way, I would ponder the meaning of death and the soul.

My parents tried to give their children formal religious training. My brother and I attended Jewish Sunday school. Even though they insisted that my brother have a bar mitzvah, neither their hearts nor their temperaments were suited to rigid theology. I had been raised Reform, which, in the Jewish faith, is considered barely being Jewish at all. The more Orthodox branches of my religion grudgingly admit that we believe in God, although they wonder if we have trouble remembering His name.

My religious training can best be summed up as hit-and-miss, and though we celebrated the holidays of my faith, God was treated just like an easygoing patriarch, without the customary obedience and reverence He was accorded in more Orthodox homes. My mother held firm to the belief that the soul was eternal and that you could reach God no matter where you were or what you'd done. My dad also believed that each individual had a direct line of prayer to God. Having been a prisoner of war (POW), my father had learned the importance of individuality and inner strength, and, added to his natural streak of rebellion, he had no interest in any religion that was organized and tidy. He was convinced that once the more base and basic of man's foibles got involved, religion and its dogma lost the fundamental foundation of love.

My parents' beliefs pushed open the doors to my own youthful exploration, which reached its pseudointellectual zenith when I was fourteen and pompously wrote a school paper that stated with certainty that religion is nothing more than an opiate for the masses (as Karl Marx called it), a crutch to avoid confronting the finality of death. With all the conviction of youth, I stated that "true strength" was to face and acknowledge that this life is all there is, and that the universe is benignly indifferent to our little piping dreams, and that we all eventually become dust. At this age, I considered myself quite the expert on death, having devoured the works of heavyweights such as Elie Wiesel, Albert Camus, Franz Kafka, and Jean-Paul Sartre. The result of all this was that, while my contemporaries busied themselves sniffing out a date for the prom, I poured my energies into waving a flag for existentialism.

I realize now that I was one of those annoying teenagers who figured that if a word had enough syllables in it, it had to be deep, and I grabbed a seat on that bandwagon. Soon I came around again, this time with Hermann Hesse. Growing up in a household where the Almighty was so malleable, fluid, and unboxed by doctrine, it didn't take any great leap of imagination on my part to assign myself the role of His assistant.

It was a safe and loving hole for me to climb into. I never believed that my parents ever really heard me. I felt I had to prove them wrong by justifying my existence. I couldn't conceive of a showier, more exalted position to land than being the messenger of God. I told no one of my new calling, realizing that my mission was best kept under wraps until the proper moment when God and I were ready to spring it on the world.

But like an envelope stamped and ready to mail—and then overlooked and forgotten—the moment my father would walk through the front door, all was right with the world. I wisely chose not to discuss my bedroom revelation with my parents, as they were too busy struggling their way through this life to pay much attention to whatever may come after.

My mother's concern was paying the grocer's bill, while my father spent sleepless nights wondering why women across America were suddenly no longer wanting to wear housecoat dresses. My father's business predicament wasn't that he always found himself in the wrong place at the wrong time. It was more heartbreaking than that. He always seemed to land in the right place just as the right time was ending.

I would put down my bombastic revelation to a child's flight of fancy soaring out of a lagoon of loneliness if not for the emotions it stirred within me. Those emotions still exist, but no longer as shields to protect me from a reality too cold and harsh to deal with. Over the years, they've solidified into a belief system that encompasses all the realities that life has to offer.

What I had unknowingly unearthed was an innate belief system that there was a very real and definite connective tissue that binds us to the unseen world, where hearts and minds travel after their stay on this planet has been completed. This was my first connection with that gossamer thing we call the soul. Let's see an imaginary friend do that!

Perhaps all of the emotional contortions I put myself through could have been avoided had my mother scooped me up in her arms and given me warm kisses of understanding. Maybe if my father had not left so many times on business without saying good-bye. Perhaps he thought this silent departure would be easier on me, or, with his own ego in such a fragile state, maybe he thought I wouldn't notice. I don't know. Maybe it was all just to keep me in communion with heaven. When you are that lonely, you rely on what love there is—even if you cannot see it.

I do know, as the cliché so aptly puts it, you can't un-ring a bell. But there does come a time when we have to stop listening to the clanging in our ears. I don't blame any aftermath my emotions may have suffered on their actions or lack thereof. As I have learned since giving birth, parenthood is not an exact science, and no matter how pure and positive your intentions, the odds of actually hitting your mark are somewhere below that of bowling or darts.

Alas, I didn't have the necessary overview at that time. I

would spend angry hours in my room, teaching myself to hate and separate. No living organism on earth can feel as sorry for itself as a child, and I used my private world as a tether of seething anger to connect me to my family. This lifeline of alienation was exactly that, and I no longer minded the vague and distant connection I felt, because now it was on my terms. In my longing, my needing, my seething, and my dreaming, I began to understand the negative form of connection.

Unconsciously, the worst parts of me slowly became the genesis of my strength. As I look back at that little girl, holed up in her room like a caterpillar in a cocoon, I see now that transforming my emotions was a necessary survival technique. I developed a rich fantasy life as I became independent, self-sufficient, and strong. Then I reached the inevitable crossroads. Somewhere inside I knew that, for true survival, hate can only get you so far until it eats away like acid. I needed to overcome why I was so afraid of love.

Do we really know other people, or do we only know ourselves from the reaction we feel when we're around them? How are we really to know the parts of ourselves that we suppress? If we emotionally keep ourselves separate, then how is it possible to know who we truly are? Alone in my tiny bedroom, I asked myself all of these questions, although I didn't realize it at the time. I was lonely, not profound.

Children work best with basic emotions, not intricate, grand designs. Although their feelings may often be dramatic and outstretched, the core of those emotions is often pitch-perfect. If my own juvenile sensibilities were universal, as I believe they were, perhaps it's this early time of life as we listen intently to hear and understand ourselves not in connection to others but in opposition and rebellion. After all, to be in resistance is to inherently understand who we are against structure.

And if that tack didn't work and I went along and didn't rock the boat, then I swallowed my rebellion along with everything else—I overate. As the years clicked on and my parents' intake of alcohol and pills rose to a frightening level, I became an embryonic philosopher inside the womblike safety of my bedroom. Locked up alone with my thoughts wouldn't have been my first choice of how I would have liked to travel through puberty, but it was still preferable to knowing with certainty that no one was paying attention to me.

When I was sixteen years old, an age when most girls are deciding which turtleneck sweater to wear to cover up their latest hickey, I discovered that I was psychic. Perhaps I had better clarify—whenever the word "psychic" is uttered, one's thoughts immediately conjure up crystal balls and hoop earrings. For me, psychic ability is nothing more than freeing us enough to allow our senses to walk the high wire of an often-unused wavelength.

There can be no question that a variety of ways of communicating with our surroundings exists. Dogs do it with their keen sense of smell, while bats wing their way around navigated by echolocation. I have often wondered if the reason mankind created language was because, as evolution kept upping the ante of our brainpower, our other senses were forced to take a backseat and eventually atrophied from lack of use. This is just my opinion, certainly, but I do believe we got the worst of that trade.

So, to me, there is nothing mystical or otherworldly inherent in the word "psychic." It is simply walking down the path of what Robert Frost would have described as "the road not taken." That doesn't mean that road doesn't exist. It simply means that it's been covered over with brambles and vines from lack of foot traffic.

So there I was, alone in my room, when the name Tim Sharpe popped into my head. He was Miami Beach High's star of the football team as well as student body president. He was one of those rare teenagers who a girl of sixteen and her parents could both love. I was in tenth grade. Tim Sharpe was a senior, and he wasn't part of my world. That was why it came as such a shock, though a pleasant one, that he should suddenly burst his way into my thoughts one night as I plowed slowly through algebra. I noted the out-of-nowhere feeling.

The next night he called me and asked me out on a date.

I can only surmise that Tim must have been thinking of asking me out at the exact same moment he crashed into my consciousness. I realized there are senders and there are receivers. We are connected. (This isn't the place to go into detail about how the date went, other than to say that I wore a turtleneck to school the following Monday.)

Puberty for both sexes is a bumpy road of self-doubt, where the flesh of our identity is suddenly altered. For me it came between the ages of ten and eleven, when my breasts suddenly made their abundant appearance (from a training bra to a DD size). The last thing a young girl wants to do is stick out, and nothing sticks out more than big breasts on an eleven-year-old.

Crossing the physical bridge from childhood to woman-hood is never easy, but it can be devastating when you cross too early. You become a freak, an oddity, and the object of the kind of cold, heartless ridicule only children are cruel enough to dish out. I taught myself little tricks. I slumped. I carried my schoolbooks pressed against my chest. My tricks didn't hide my breasts but only revealed my embarrassment and humilia-tion. I wished I had a mother I could confide in, but even she seemed to be against me, silently viewing my blossoming phys-icality as a threat to her own sexuality. So when Tim asked me out, it was as if he was offering me a helping hand back into a world of acceptance I had long ago believed was lost to me.

Around the same time, I began to toy with the idea of a sixth sense beyond the tangible top five when I stumbled onto one of my father's old *Playboy* magazines. (This was back in the day when even skin magazines had a sense of decorum, and the female pubic area remained as mysterious as the Bermuda Tri-angle.) I quickly thumbed through the pictorials, wondering if the amply endowed women gracing the pages had gone through the same hell I had, then suddenly stopped when I reached their monthly in-depth interview, this time with Dr. Elisabeth Kübler-Ross. She had become famous for her book *On Death and Dying*, in which she listed the "five psychological stages of dying":

denial, anger, bargaining, depression, and acceptance.

I remember the interviewer noted that she smoked one cigarette after another. He challenged her by asking how, as someone who works with cancer patients, she could justify her continuous chain-smoking. Kübler-Ross replied that if she had to die, she would much rather have cancer than get hit by a car, because a cancer patient is often afforded the time to make resolutions with the ones they love.

She told of how, when she sat bedside with dying patients, she would hear them talking to those around them who didn't exist. The patient often used specific names, and when Kübler-Ross would inquire about those mentioned with family members, they confirmed that the various monikers belonged to those of deceased family members. Following in the footsteps of one of her heroes, Dr. Raymond Moody, she began to research life after life.

When I opened that issue of *Playboy*, I was merely curious, a very young woman comparing breasts and beauty with my own self-image. When I closed the magazine, my perceptions of the world of souls was substantiated, confirmed, and ratified forever. Doctors actually researching what I secretly held dearest would take my life down paths I had never imagined possible.

I no longer saw my future within the four walls of the bedroom. Now it was what I couldn't see that interested me most.

Chapter Two

California, Here I Come

Hollywood is a place where there is no definition
of your worth earlier than your last picture.

MURRAY KEMPTON

FOR THE FIRST TIME IN MEMORY, I awoke before my alarm
clock had a chance to buzz and badger me from sleep. I knew the
life-altering importance of this morning's job interview. I had to
be careful which clothes I picked to wear. My wardrobe had to
be a reflection of all the attributes I was certain they would want
in an employee. My goal was to appear intelligent and earnest.

And I wanted to be sexy.

In the household where I grew up, the sensuality that crack-
led between my parents was palpable and highly charged. My

13

mother was French and had been a model, and the pilot light that warmed her sexuality was always on. The French have a way of turning a simple smile into an erotic overture, and as a child I would sit and watch her carefully apply her makeup, each dab like a stroke from an artist's brush. I was transfixed.

My feelings changed over time, as time was my mother's great enemy. She had built her house of self-esteem on her looks, and as they started to fade, there were no other building blocks where her fragile ego could take refuge. I carved a mental note that I would never lock myself inside the same predicament.

Now I found myself doing everything I'd watched my mother do when I was a child. I prettied and preened, and had a fashion show in front of my full-length mirror, trying on everything I owned to examine how I looked from every seductive angle. After much deliberation I finally decided to go with a white, gauzy, Indian cotton dress with a big, red, wide belt. I dabbed on just the right amount of makeup, sprayed on a hint of perfume, and finished putting this package together by pushing my baby-fine, straight hair to one side with a barrette. (I never did know exactly what to do with my hair.) When I was a child, my mother's mother would toss compliments over me like confetti, and then pop my ego by telling me how sad it was that I was cursed with hair that sat limply on top of my head.

An hour later I was sitting across the desk from Michael Rosenfeld, who interviewed all potential employees for Creative Artists Agency (CAA), the newest talent agency in Hollywood.

As I sat there nervously, I watched as his eyes took me in

from head to toe. Then he said, with an uncanny knack for turning a compliment into an interrogation, "You are way too sexy." At twenty-three, I couldn't help but be momentarily flattered. This was a long-standing pattern. In times of heightened anxiety, which this certainly was, the more flirtatious I unconsciously became.

It was 1976, and the women's movement had by then sprinted past, with adherents tossing bras into bonfires and debating on the more substantial arena of abortion rights and equal pay.

"Don't you know the days of women acting like men are passé? Men love feminine women," I said. "There is a new day here, where sexy women can still have moxie, be successfully brazen, assertive, and effective."

My display of righteous feminine grit caught him off guard, but his reaction seemed to be one of mild amusement. He gave me a half smile and called me "formidable." Then he quickly took it away by saying, "Cute, too," and then told me to "stay in touch."

I was too inexperienced to realize that meant nothing other than the meeting was over. I decided to take him at his word and called his office once a week wondering if I could get that second meeting. I was determined to become a Hollywood agent, an occupation I hadn't given so much as a moment's thought to just a few months ago.

Miami Beach was my hometown, but once a year it morphed into a bikini-clad magnet for eastern university students in need of a little sun, surf, and seduction to get them through the remainder of their education. I was seventeen when I met Jeff King, proving that kismet can happen when you least expect it, even in Miami Beach during spring break. Jeff attended New York University (NYU) to study film. At that time, the idea of sitting in a classroom to study film was an unappreciated, new, and radical concept. As I listened to Jeff, I immediately imagined a way to meld my love for both art and psychology into creating images for the screen.

Somehow, as I excitedly mapped out my future plans for my father, he didn't quite embrace the comet that was to be my Hollywood career. My father came from the generation where dreams had no choice but to take a backseat to bringing in a weekly paycheck. Living through the Depression can do that to you. Money—or lack thereof—was the driving engine that determined every family decision. It seemed that no matter how many hours he poured into his job, my dad could never make a consistent living in Florida real estate, which always teetered on the verge of crashing, at least in our household. As a child, I could always tell how unsuccessful his day had been by the width of the perspiration circles beneath his armpits—and by the number of Scotches he poured for himself when he got home.

When I gushed my future plans to my father, I should have realized what his reaction would be. His answer was to grab the current copy of *TV Guide* and wave it in front of me with the same solemnity that Moses grasped the Ten Commandments and held them up for the Israelites to behold. The cover read

"Hollywood: Drugs, Sex, Divorce." My father was not about to allow his sweet, innocent daughter to dive headfirst into this diseased cesspool of debauchery. (Like many parents, the bar of moral standards he set for me was a good deal higher than the one he set for himself.)

My instinct was to argue or, if necessary, throw a tantrum, but I realized there was no way to fight *TV Guide*. At the end of this primarily one-sided conversation, he decided to dangle a carrot. He promised that, after I received my associate's degree, if I still wanted to go to film school, I could transfer. I took him at his word, although I would have felt better about the oath had he said it with his right hand pointing to God and his left hand placed firmly on *TV Guide*.

I had done my homework—the two best film schools were NYU and the University of Southern California (USC). I leaned toward NYU, with the idea of getting a small apartment in the Village, although I wasn't sure exactly where that was. It didn't matter, as it had always sounded to me like a place where somehow it was romantic to be young and poor and struggling.

Unfortunately, my father was from New York, and he insisted the Village was too rough, where drugs and sexual aberrations were to be found on every street corner. I realize now that it was my father's mission in life to keep his little girl from going any-where that Lenny Bruce had ever been.

My dad could really sell when he had to. (It was just our bad luck that the only thing he couldn't successfully peddle was Florida real estate.) "You know, Florida State has a campus in

Florence, Italy," he said, artfully dangling another carrot. "For no extra tuition we could send you to Europe to study art history."

He scrutinized my face as I did my best to appear as if I was weighing my options, putting the same wrinkles in my forehead that I would try so hard to remove after I hit forty.

I really didn't want to put off the promised land of film school, but, after all, Florence, Italy, didn't roll around every day. At least it didn't in my household. I agreed, as he knew I would. I'm a sucker for a good carrot.

After landing in Florence, I unpacked and immediately got a job working in the school library. (Europe tried to sell Americans on the metric system while we tried to get them excited over the Dewey decimal system. They were both doomed to fail.) I didn't know anyone, I had no familiar landmarks to grasp in comfortable recognition, and I couldn't understand the language. I never felt quite so alone in my life as I did those first few weeks. All that was left to me were my powers of observation, which, I came to realize years later, is the backbone of all intuition and good filmmaking.

I'd been brought up in an environment where sitting up straight and not putting your elbows on the table were of great importance. Italians were different. The people were jovial and embracing. They seemed to put a higher premium on the simple pleasures rather than on money, power, and fame, the triple crown of achievement that Americans so often chase.

Europe, I quickly discovered, is all about the past. The Renaissance was Florence's heyday, and anything that happened after those glory days came to an end didn't appear to have much staying power. It was a far cry from Miami Beach, where the population seemed to be older than the surroundings.

I had a wonderful time, but I can't say that anything I learned truly stuck to my intellectual ribs. The trouble with college, it would seem, is that it's trying to educate an age group that believes it already knows everything. By 1974, I'd had my fill of all things dead and returned to the states, where I entered USC as a junior in cinema production. I wanted to be a film director. My father, realizing that I was every inch as bullheaded as he was, had finally made good on his long-ago promise. Maybe he had run out of carrots to dangle.

Like my fellow film school students, I smoldered with earnestness. Our duty, we believed, was to keep ourselves emotionally open, ready to unzip our deepest secrets and share them in the hopes of being able to reveal life's mysteries. (We were all young, remember, and so unraveling a few of life's more important mysteries didn't seem like such a tough nut to crack.)

In film school we would split off into groups. Celluloid is one of the most collaborative of mediums; we learned quickly to rely on each other's creativity, particularly on days when our own brilliance couldn't manage to get out of bed.

We worked in a think tank. The group would wrestle with a specific story problem, getting nowhere slowly and finally falling into exhausted silence. During those silences, an idea seemed to drift down from the skies and choose one of our numbed heads to enter. There was something serendipitous about the whole process, and although we didn't discuss it, it was as if in our silence, we took on the role of middlemen and received ideas that were bigger than ourselves.

That's the high road of film school. The low road is the tangled swamp of egos you have to try and cut your way through. I'm sure that mine bulged as much as all the others. I like to believe I was more polite about it. My good manners, I'm embarrassed to admit, were well thought out with an eye toward the future. Success in the film business is often built on friendships and derailed by enemies. I wasn't about to make enemies out of anyone who might someday be able to offer me a helping hand up the ladder to my goal.

Ego is a necessary character trait of anyone who believes that their ideas are worth flickering inside every theater in every mall across America. That said, immature egos are the worst, as they still have something to prove and don't believe they have the luxury to be wrong.

Although not mentioned in any curriculum, this may be the most important lesson I learned in film school: how to let raging egos flash and collide without allowing it to turn into a bloodbath of temperament. I preferred to leave people with their dignity. I always knew there had to be a better way; I just hadn't figured it out yet.

Twenty-three years old and just minutes out of film school, I was ready to take the town by storm. Exactly what I thought that storm was I have no idea. Fortunately, I quickly landed a job as a production assistant in television, pulling in the

princely sum of $500 a week. I may not have been listed in the
Forbes 400, but I wallowed in what I thought of as my meteoric
rise in show business.

My job was grunt work: laboring late into the night and
drinking bad coffee while inserting different colored rewrite
pages into the cast and crew books. When I spoke to my father,
I glowed with pride. The sorry truth was that if you looked right
beneath the low man on the totem pole, you would find me.

It didn't take long before my glow began to wear off and I
realized that I was a long, long way from the center of my aspirations. No one, it seemed, was the least bit interested in either
the honed cinematic eye or bulging creative muscle that I had
worked so hard to achieve in film school.

Then, miraculously, the same kismet that had brought me
together with Jeff in Miami Beach put another man in my path
to change the course of my already sputtering life. He was
dressed immaculately in a custom-tailored suit, smelling of
Aramis cologne and wearing Gucci loafers. I wondered what
he did, as he was obviously dressed far too impeccably to have
any talent. I was told in an awed whisper that Lee Cohen was
the packaging agent from William Morris Agency. It appeared
he could walk over to anyone and they all, no matter how busy,
found time to talk to him. That, to my inexperienced eyes,
seemed to encompass his entire job; just to walk and talk, as
well as know who was important enough to pat on the shoulder. Having caught a glimpse of the green pastures on that side
of show business, I was ready to make my career move.

I started to read the trade papers and quickly became aware that many ex-agents were now producing movies. Producer Ray Stark had been an agent. Producer Larry Turman had been an agent. In a business of nonsense, this almost seemed to make sense. Agents know the business end of show business. I now had a new goal. I wanted to be an ex-agent. (I had been the only woman and only undergraduate to direct a thesis film that year, but the film had been underwhelming. I thought my greatest feat was that I garnered the assignment. Maybe I had a knack for producing.) Of course, that meant I would have to become an agent first, an alien arena I knew nothing about and cared for even less. But it was a goal to a bigger goal, and any movement in that direction was good enough for me.

I applied to all the big agencies like William Morris and International Creative Management (ICM). I inflated my meager résumé with so much hot air I was afraid it would blow away before I got to the mailbox. When the top tier of agencies didn't exactly stampede for my services, I aimed my sights slightly lower. And then a little lower. The ladder of success, I was finding out, only works if you can get ahold of the bottom rung so you can start climbing.

Then, from out of nowhere (that unforeseeable place where the good things usually come from), I got a phone call from Michael Rosenfeld at Creative Artists Agency. Five agents had just jumped ship over at William Morris to form their own company, which was nicknamed CAA around town, at least by the few people who had heard of them. Forming a new agency is always a dicey venture, regardless of the brains involved, and no one questioned that among the five they had some of the most active brain cells in the business. Still, as far as crapshoots go, this ran neck and neck alongside the Irish Sweepstakes. But at that point it was all I had to pin my future hopes to.

In Los Angeles we have a rainy season, where all the rain for the entire year seems to crash down on the town in a few short weeks. It's the same way with lucky breaks. As I peppered Michael Rosenfeld with phone calls about my future, I heard from ICM, one of the behemoths of the agency business. My résumé had caught their attention. At that time ICM was the biggest shark following in William Morris's wake. And for some unfathomable reason, they saw me as a tasty bit of chum.

It was an easy decision. At least it should have been. ICM had stood at the summit of the agency business for years, while in all likelihood CAA would prove to be just another comet flashing temporarily over the Hollywood skies before hurling itself into oblivion. I knew the right thing to do; the smart thing to do. It was what years later would be referred to as a "no-brainer." But when it came to making any of life's big choices, my brain never acted alone. I was green at being psychic, but I knew enough to arm wrestle with my gut instinct before any final decision was reached.

My gut instinct saw my future at CAA.

In this instance, my brain finally agreed with it. ICM was an ocean liner compared to this new little dinghy of a company. But it's a lot easier to rise to the rank of admiral on a dinghy.

After all, I would be working alongside the principals of CAA. And I did believe in them. They were hungrier. They were younger.

As I continued to debate with myself, I received a real offer from ICM, forcing me into an immediate resolution. I finally decided to leave my future up to fate, always the final arbiter after my brain and gut instinct have battled for twelve pounding rounds without a decision being reached. I dashed off a telegram to CAA, laced with what I hoped was humor, and said I needed an answer as ICM was after my services.

As I'd hoped, Michael Rosenfeld quickly replied, because in Hollywood there is nothing that makes you more desirable than when someone else wants to hire you. He told me that my next interview was to be with Mike Ovitz, the head of this minuscule juggernaut that was hell-bent on taking over the town.

Rosenfeld advised me to wear a dark, tailored, men's-style suit, pull my hair back into a ponytail, not to wear any makeup, and to carry a briefcase. I was tempted to ask him if I should drop my voice a couple of octaves, but again, my hunch spoke up—don't be a smart-ass. But I knew he was right. Even then, the Hollywood power brokers were always most comfortable with what they had already seen.

In 1976 there were very few women of power in the film industry, and I chose to wait to rock the boat until after I had actually gotten into it. I dressed as I was told, although underneath the prescribed uniform, I did wear my most feminine bra and panties, if only to remind myself of the soft curves the suit covered. As I drove toward CAA to meet with Mike Ovitz for the first and perhaps last time, I was filled with the tonic of confidence. I knew I was doing the right thing, although my father had raised objections as loudly and as strongly as he could.

By this time I'd been promoted to an associate producer position. It was impossible for him to fathom why his daughter would walk away from a $700-per-week job for one that paid only $150. I tried to make him understand that an agent was a career choice, not a freelance independent contractor, but my reasoning was beyond his life experience. Quite simply, I was doing what I would continue to do when the roads of my life diverged—I would trust in instinct to somehow reach the future that my heart had mapped out for it.

Chapter Three

What Do You Say to a Thousand-Pound Gorilla?

Omnipotence is bought by ceaseless fear.

BLAISE PASCAL

MIKE OVITZ IS A GENIUS.

With that said I doubt whether, if Plato, Einstein, and Shakespeare met Ovitz for drinks at the Polo Lounge, the three of them would walk away saying, "Thank God, we've finally found a fourth for bridge."

That is not to say that Mike doesn't possess what can be termed an almost supernova brilliance. It's just necessary to understand that what constitutes genius in show business is made up of a completely different set of criteria than in the real world. In my view for better or worse, Mike Ovitz altered the

Hollywood universe with a modicum of talent and a maximum of willpower and ego. In the movie community, that's more than enough to earn the label "genius."

Back in the seventies, Ovitz, a young talent agent at the William Morris Agency, along with four of his equally ambitious coworkers, decided to flee those hallowed halls and head for greener pastures in their own little shop on Wilshire Boulevard. Trekking along on the Ovitz exodus were agents Ron Meyer, Bill Haber, Rowland Perkins, and Michael Rosenfeld. Joining them in their little agency incubator were agents Martin Baum and Tony Ludwig and trainee Amy Grossman, along with a few secretaries and an accounting clerk, Laverne Dennis, who was added to the mix just in case they were able to get some sort of cash flow going.

It was a minor mutiny that would have been quickly forgotten had they not carried with them a nugget of an idea that would completely revolutionize the entire film industry. Until the inception of Creative Artists Agency, the agency business conducted itself very much like the Mafia: Powerful titans in black suits puffing long cigars were content to blend invisibly into the woodwork, and pulled the strings from the safety of their chosen shadows. And, like any good mafioso chieftain, the last thing they wanted to see in the morning with their first cup of coffee was their name in the newspaper. Invisibility was a key element to a long and successful career.

The germ of genius Mr. Ovitz and company had hatched was packaging. True, packaging had always been done in one form or another, but they created a new design based simply on "the person who has the material and puts it together has the control."

"Control" was the real "C" in CAA.

That was still a few years away and not the Mike Ovitz or the Creative Artists Agency I would meet that day at their Christmas party. (Actually it was the Christmas party for puppeteers Sid and Marty Kroft, who were kind enough to allow this tiny band of renegade agents to join in their holiday festivities, as CAA was still too fledgling to purchase tinsel without throwing their ledger sheet completely out of whack.)

The Mike Ovitz I met for the first time was shy and socially ill at ease. As I later learned, he was always more comfortable behind a desk, like a pilot who only feels truly himself when at the controls of a plane. As I discovered after spending some time in the business, most people with impressive reputations are not that impressive when you actually meet them. Their very human traits have a way of overshadowing their accomplishments when up close, and the attributes we so admired from a distance become hard to spot behind a childish temper or galloping ego.

Mike Ovitz sipped eggnog while he asked me questions and I blithered out my answers. His future may have been as dicey as my own, but still, he was certainly dressed for success, wearing a dark Alandales suit and those same Hollywood Gucci loafers. If Hollywood is by nature shallow, then the reasoning goes you had better cover the only layer you've got with some great clothes.

Success. Power. Money. This is what CAA wanted to attain, and perhaps this is why, against my father's dire warnings, I wanted to grab hold. It was my dream too. Growing up I saw what failure could do. My parents' blistering arguments always centered on money and my father's inability to make it in any quantities that didn't quickly vanish into the necessities of daily living. My mother would allow her frustration to storm in his direction, but like many Floridians, he simply battened down the hatches and waited for the hurricane to pass. I wondered why his masculine pride would allow him to take it, but he would look at me and reply with a simple wink, whispering, "Hey, I just might get lucky tonight."

My father understood adversity. There were times I believed he wouldn't truly know how to function without it. Each and every important relationship in his life seemed to divide itself equally between love and hate. He was the baby in his family, adored by his mother, and because all the love tipped in his direction, he was mercilessly teased by his half sister and half brothers.

In World War II he was captured and thrown into a POW camp. My father refused to deny who and what he was. He told the Germans he was Jewish and was tortured. He had to survive for more than a year on whatever he could find. Often it turned out to be the flesh of prison rats.

Although his business partners were like trusted brothers, they would steal from the company whenever my father's back was turned. I don't know if my father was a failure in his own eyes, but there were enough eyes around him that viewed him that way for it to have had a devastating effect. The emotional temperature inside our house was in constant flux, and though I wasn't yet old enough to know what a normal household was like, I longed to feel safe and warm and protected.

When I was five years old, Mrs. Greenberg, my kindergarten teacher, poured the warm syrup of praise over me, telling my mother how pinchably cute I was, then asking her in mock seriousness if she could take me home with her. I'm sure this was a standard line she fed to all the parents, but I was too young to know the difference between a passing compliment and a concrete offer, and I immediately piped up, bellowing a joyful "Okay!" In gleeful anticipation of the upcoming exchange, I turned to my mother, only to see that my ecstatic outburst had caused her smile to quickly crumble into heartbreaking pain. My immediate reply even surprised me, and I was suddenly awakened to how much I hated my home life.

When as a child I would hide in my bedroom and listen as my mother pummeled my father with verbal lightning bolts, I was convinced that my father was a weak man. But a child often views her parents through a kaleidoscope of shifting emotions, and as I grew older I finally came to realize that it was all about love—their version of it.

This was finally confirmed many years later when my father was dying and I asked him what he thought his purpose on this earth was. I can't imagine a bigger question, but he was able to answer it succinctly and without a moment's hesitation: "I tried to love my wife and my children as much as possible," he said. The grand simplicity of his reply remains the best and most heartfelt understanding I've ever heard of our purpose here on earth.

But I knew the pain all those years of failure had carved into his heart. I promised myself I wouldn't allow it to happen to me. Success. Power. Money. Maybe those would bring happiness. I had no firsthand knowledge what joys that mighty triumvirate could bring, but I had a steely determination to find out.

After the eggnog and the interview were both drained dry, Mike Ovitz gave me a hearty handshake and I gave him a hearty handshake in return (considering the mannish manner in which I was dressed, it seemed appropriate). As we pumped hands, I was told I had the job on persistence alone. I naturally took this as a compliment, but driving home I realized that also meant he saw absolutely nothing else in me worth hiring. I decided not to dwell on that sore point, as I was capable within the hour of turning this victory into a major crisis of self-worth. Instead I mentally chose to celebrate the fact that I was now an agent, which was halfway to my dream of becoming an ex-agent.

Landing this job soon proved out. CAA quickly became the most powerful agency in Hollywood. Over the following years my gut instinct would have a lot to answer for. Still, I don't want to give my intuitive abdomen all of the blame.

Being psychic, you'd have thought I could have seen what was coming.

Chapter Four

Drafted into the Sexual
Revolution . . . Reluctantly

*The sexual embrace can only be compared
with music and with prayer.*

MARCUS AURELIUS

MY GENERATION DIDN'T DISCOVER SEX, but we certainly carried on as if we did. When I say "we," I'm putting my name on the guest list of a party to which I arrived embarrassingly late.

I was one of the baby boomers who grew up screaming at the Beatles and dedicating myself to remolding the world between campus demonstrations. As the cliché goes, the world was our oyster, and we had every intention of slurping it down in one glorious gulp.

Mine was perhaps the last generation where girls were

33

brought up truly believing that their virginity was a gift, to be handed over to the right man only on their wedding night. (I have since learned that nothing can put a crimp into a really fun evening like virginity, but myths often carry a greater weight than truths.) When I sailed haphazardly through puberty, girls belonged to one of two socially defined camps: the "good girls" who rigorously halted backseat affection somewhere below the neck and above the breasts and the ones who were classified as "easy." These girls were branded with a "reputation" and were a target for locker room snickering and braggadocio from all the males who couldn't get a date on Saturday night and were also most likely closet virgins.

When the sexual revolution exploded, somewhere around the time of *Sgt. Pepper's Lonely Hearts Club Band*, women considered themselves suddenly free of the restraints of their parents and society and began wearing love beads instead of underwear. (How we thought either of these fashion statements would bring the Vietnam War to an end quicker, I, thankfully, don't remember.)

I hung on to my virginity longer than most, to the point where it became embarrassing, like dragging a trail of toilet paper around with you on the bottom of your shoe. Whether true or not, being a virgin began to feel similar to how it felt to be a "tramp" only a few years earlier, and you were positive that you were now the object of jokes and derision.

Although I clung desperately to my virginity like a drowning woman hangs on to a buoy, two of my greatest loves happened when I was still in high school. Both of these relationships were immaculately platonic and set the course of my life, and still impact me to this day. David Abramowitz was the conservative rabbi's son. Unlike most boys in their teens who seem to be almost embarrassed by their intellectual pursuits, David had a thirst to follow his thoughts in any and all directions they took him.

Outside of class there were few other students who were eager to delve into life's mysteries with him. In me he found a zealous participant. While our contemporaries would give their nights over to make-out sessions, David and I would spend countless hours mulling over T. S. Eliot, Thomas Mann, and the mysticism in Judaism, and hoping that together we would finally crack the eternal riddle of what God is. After all, "Israel" means "one who wrestles with God" (Genesis 32:28). To the best of my recollection, we never unearthed any answers, but the questions in themselves proved to be exhilarating.

While Rabbi Mayer Abramowitz was giving his Shabbat services, David and I huddled together in the rabbi's study kissing. David and I were truly inseparable, like two yolks occupying the same egg. I would be at his house into the late evenings. After a long, tiring Saturday of services, his father would pull a sweatshirt over his pajamas, grab the two of us, and take us out for pancakes. As we passed the syrup, his father would grill me on my knowledge of Judaism. The rabbi would look long and hard into my eyes with a knowing that, as much as they both loved me, it could never work out. As he put it succinctly, with his slight Israeli accent to David, "Dovey, she eats too many oysters."

First love is a monumentally defining flash point in one's youth. Even as David and I began drifting away from each other and into our own maturity, I assessed how much, someday, I wanted a man like David. But in some deep, fundamental part of me, I knew that his father was right, and that I wasn't going to be the long-term woman for him. As inquisitive as I may have been, when it got down to the nitty-gritty of religion, I would never be impressive when it came to observing Jewish law.

My best friend in high school was Ellen Zisquit, a "Fummy" Orthodox Jew. Dinner at her house was always a joyous, animated affair, where we would get into lively Talmudic debates over kosher brisket. (This is where I learned not to attempt to make a conversational point after just eating a forkful of horseradish.) Meals at my house often were bristling in their silence, and I gratefully latched onto Ellen and her parents and turned them into my surrogate family. I loved their Orthodox home. I listened and learned as ideas flew across the table. They taught me to lovingly debate, and even more than that, they gave the still waters of my life meaning.

Unlike my own family, the Zisquit clan could banter without their sabers rattling. Sometimes they disagreed just for the sheer joy of a lively pursuit of clarity. From David and Ellen and the warm bosom of their families, I learned how deep and rich and thoughtful love could really be. Yet, by the time I got into college, I still hadn't done much experimenting with the more tactile kind.

When I was in my twenties and certain that I was the only one among my peers who "hadn't done it," I decided it was time to take the plunge, or, more precisely, find the right boy who I'd allow to do just that. As I had felt the pressure to hang on to my virginity, now I felt the pressure to lose it. The actual event was mechanical and melancholy. There was the usual fumbling and bumbling that occurs at such an awkward time, and though he rushed through it as most boys his age do, it couldn't be over too quick for me. Not only did the earth not move, we didn't do a lot of moving either.

I approached losing my virginity the way one does going to the dentist, and when it was over, the last thing I wanted to think about was my next appointment. Adding to my future reluctance was when I discovered shortly afterward that the boy I chose to lose my virginity to already had a girlfriend, and I was no more than exactly what I wanted to avoid, a quickie conquest. Naturally, I was both wounded and humiliated, but I can't say that I was surprised. I was brought up believing that all men cheat. My father enveloped me with his love and affection, at least for those all-too-brief intervals when he was home. But as a traveling salesman, he was on the road a lot. And when he was on the road, he was seldom lonely.

How I came to know that he was more interested in the ladies than in the ladies' dresses he was selling, I don't remember. Certainly no one sat me down and discussed my father's infidelities with me. I can only imagine that whiffs of his other life came to me through every child's greatest tool of learning:

eavesdropping. My parents would argue behind closed doors, but their bitterness couldn't help but drift throughout the house and seep into the sponge of my consciousness.

Children can't define adultery, and even if they could, it would be impossible for them to grasp its full meaning. But I knew instinctively that whatever my beloved father had done when he was away had clawed at and shredded my mother's heart. She was French. They were raised to take it.

Now that I was, at last, a full and complete woman, with my virginity finally over and done with, I would unconsciously continue the cycle I witnessed in my childhood. I entered the adult world already jaded to the mirage of true and lasting love, convinced that all men were basically unfaithful scoundrels and women only survived by looking somewhere besides their husbands for that constant source of fulfillment that's so necessary to get us from one day to the next. I looked to show business, my dream of making films, and my evolving belief system that life didn't end with our final breath.

A few years' worth of women's lib can't erase all the thousands of years Nature had taken to set up the basic male-female relationship. To keep the species rolling, men are wired to spread their seeds merrily around. While on the distaff side, women are wired to raise those seeds until they get jobs and move out of the house. When we finally reached womanhood, our sex, in a show of lusty bravado, thought the passport to true liberation was to act more like men. We did our damnedest to convince ourselves that meaningless sex was to our liking, but women have never been in happy sync with the meaningless. We give birth, raise offspring, and keep the home fires forever burning. There isn't time or taste for the meaningless.

The last thing I was thinking about when I began working at Creative Artists Agency was marriage. My commitment was to myself and the dreams I had mapped out for my future.

I've never been very good with maps. It was early in my days at CAA when I agreed to a date with a man I knew I should do everything in my power to avoid. He was young, tall, and good-looking, with the kind of intelligence that can be daunting if all of your brain cells aren't on their toes.

His one and only drawback was that he was then training to be an agent at William Morris. This cross-pollinating may not seem like much outside Hollywood, but in the agency business it was akin to marrying outside your species. Pillow talk was thought to take on a particularly nefarious nature when agents from competing companies were doing the talking.

I knew Jack Rapke slightly. Our paths had already crossed, if only because our backgrounds were so uncannily similar: Jewish from Miami, poor childhoods, and film school.

Jack had his heart set on becoming a director, and, like me, had decided to become an agent as a stepping-stone to financial security and future glory behind the camera. Dating a man so much like me seemed like a perfect way to avoid any possible future arguments. It wouldn't prove true, of course. I had somehow managed to forget that all of my most vicious disagreements had taken place within myself.

Jack and I discreetly made a date to get together, but he had to cancel at the last minute. Business. Another date, another cancellation. More business. This happened five times. After the third time, my pride was embarrassed to admit it even knew me. But I forged ahead, doing what I did best; I rationalized. We were in the same line of work, after all, and both planted firmly at the bottom of the barrel in our respective companies. When you're in that particular lowly position, your private life must always be put on hold when you're asked to do something, no matter how seemingly trivial.

First dates are tricky, at best. You only want to illuminate those aspects of your character that shine a positive light on your personality, and hope that those areas of yourself that you haven't gotten a chance to work on yet don't seep through before dessert arrives. I would be fun, but thoughtful. Witty, yet serious. And, above all, I would be interesting. If a second date is ever going to materialize, an intelligent man has to be with a woman who can poke at his gray matter as well as his libido.

I needn't have bothered.

Before we could get our linen napkins draped over our laps Jack began to talk about himself, and when that conversation ended, he talked about himself some more. I was beginning to wish we'd had this date the night when it had been originally slated. That way it would have been over by now.

It was the appetizers that changed the date and the course of my life.

Knowing how little money he was making, I declined his

invitation to order an appetizer and asked for an entrée. He wouldn't hear of it. He insisted. Nothing I could say would get me out of ordering an appetizer. I debated: Should we share the clams casino or the stuffed mushroom caps? Jack solved my culinary dilemma by calling the waiter over and grandly ordering both.

Realizing that this could financially eliminate a couple of his lunches for the following week, I was deeply touched by the gesture. Together we forked our way through the clams casino and stuffed mushroom caps. After that I don't remember the entrée or what we talked about. What I do remember is that we closed the place, and a few heady weeks later, Jack and I were living together. Jack seemed to have all the attributes I wanted in the man I was certain I would share the rest of my life with. At twenty-seven he had a burning desire for both success and for me—two potent aphrodisiacs when picking out the man you want to wrap the rest of your days around. Obviously, he would be successful, as he was driven by the same fierce sense of "Success, Power, and Money" that fueled me. In a business where bad behavior is too often considered acceptable, we both tried to do our job with dignity and taste.

And most important of all, he wanted children, which was my deepest desire.

When we first started living together, we continued to keep our relationship hushed and private, and the smoky, musk-filled air of being in an illicit romance only added more heat to a fire that had already engulfed us. Jack was smart, young, and ambitious. But there was something else, something I could see in him even at times when he couldn't. Although Jack was rough around the edges, he had that most intangible of attributes: charisma.

It's possible that every woman caught helplessly in the first giant wave of love sees qualities in her man that don't really exist, but Jack lived up to all my expectations, at least career-wise, even if he didn't live up to his own. With my support and gentle nudging, after earning his agent's stripes at William Morris, Jack moved over to CAA, where he eventually became the agent of almost every important director in Hollywood.

His rapid rise wasn't a matter of luck. Wanting so desperately to be a director himself, Jack knew exactly how to talk to, relate to, and soothe that wild breed of artist. Over time, his close proximity to his dream, without ever being able to touch it, caused Jack much heartache and more than a little self-contempt. But that was still years away. He was too busy succeeding to question whether it was really the success he had wanted. The trouble with climbing the ladder quickly is that you don't stop to look back to see which important dreams you may have discarded on your rise to the top.

What could have ended as little more than a memorable fling quickly developed into a rich, vibrant bond of love, trust, and caring. The next step, a step I hadn't even considered before we shared those two appetizers, was now inevitable. Jack's mother, Magda, a woman impossible not to adore, took me by the hand to see psychics and gypsies; she was Hungarian and she "believed." (Perhaps that's why I felt so instantly comfortable with her. We were kindred spirits who truly believed in the soul.) Because Jack and I worked for competitive companies, we decided it was best to have the ceremony out of town, to avoid business contention our workers might raise. We chose Miami, as three out of our four parents lived there (Magda being the only one residing in Los Angeles).

Magda asked me which rabbi I had engaged to marry us. Naturally I had chosen my old friend Mayer Abramowitz. On hearing his name, she immediately burst into a flood of tears. "What, what?" I asked, taken aback by her surprising reaction. As mascara streaked down her cheeks, Magda explained that her brother, who had been a young rabbi chaplain in World War II, was killed at the age of twenty-six. She rummaged through a drawer and pulled out a letter that read: "Dear Magda, Your brother, Frank Goldenberg, was a tribute to not only his country, but his religion. He freed many Jews from Eastern Europe. He and I put on a Passover seder for 5,000 GIs in a Spanish castle. In his short twenty-six years he had done more for humanity than most people accomplish in a full lifetime. Signed, his best friend, Rabbi Mayer Abramowitz."

I could do little more than remain motionless, only managing to grasp her hand in my own. What was the likelihood that of all of the rabbis in the United States, I would pick the very rabbi who had been her dead brother's best friend? After that thunderbolt of a moment, I began to pay closer attention to soul groups. We come down to live out our life lessons with our soul groups. We often recognize them immediately. Sometimes we even marry them.

After Jack and I were married, our life together seemed to kick into warp speed. As our stars rose at CAA and our client lists ballooned (as well as my stomach, giving birth to Jessica and Aaron), we gave each other balance and support and advice we could trust. My only real regret is that I'm certain those days would have seemed more glamorous to me had we taken a moment to catch our breath and enjoy them.

I was passionately, madly, wildly in love. Jack was everything I'd ever wanted in a man.

And less. It was the "less" part that was so important. Love, especially when the bolt strikes you when you're in your twenties, has a blinding effect on all you thought you knew and believed in. Without even realizing it, I began closing doors on my past convictions. (This can either be good or bad, depending on those convictions.) Whether true or not, having grown up watching the twisted dynamics between my parents, I had convinced myself that it was impossible for any man to be faithful. Jack, I now assured myself, would be the glorious exception.

Chapter Five

Ronnie, My North Star

He who can, does. He who cannot, teaches.

GEORGE BERNARD SHAW

THE ABOVE IS ONE OF THE GREAT Shaw's most often quoted witticisms. With more than a little trepidation, I have to respectfully disagree with the eminent playwright and social critic.

Many of my beliefs and certainly my work ethic were formed on the bedrock of great teachers who didn't consider themselves teachers at all. Breaking with Mr. Shaw's dictum, they could do it and did—brilliantly. It was their innate need to give and to guide that made them mentors.

I was blessed to have such a person waiting for me when I

entered Creative Artists Agency for the beginning of what I hoped would be a long career.

Film school had insisted that movies were an art. CAA held fast to the attitude that movies were a business. "Sell it, don't smell it!" Ronnie would bark. They were both right.

Show business, as those two words imply, has a great regard for creativity and equal regard for the creativity of business, and it's a constant struggle to attempt to keep those two often diametrically opposed goals in some sort of balance. It has a decisively contradictory relationship with itself and can only succeed when those divergent parts can cohabitate and, finally, complement each other.

After all, the end product is not a widget, but fashioned through a concerto of human, creative collaboration that repeatedly understands that inspiration doesn't always run on schedule. Each and every element has its own unique contribution to make, and each and every element is necessary to complete the whole. The whole is a tapestry of inspiration, and the inspiration is greater than any one individual. (That, at least, is what is aspired to, though we can all rattle off a litany of less-than-stellar films that make your average widget look practically thought-provoking.)

I've always maintained, even in my darkest days, that show business is very spiritual. Hollywood is a place where giant egos still roam the earth, but even they grudgingly realize that a power greater than themselves exists. Not just because the stars must align in order for the sea to part and success is nothing short of a miracle, but because each one of us must face the void and discover a soft place within ourselves to be patient.

And it's in surrender and patience, two of the rarest of human commodities, where we find the power greater than ourselves. That void holds a knowledge that we are all indeed connected and that creativity (whether expressed artistically or through creative business) is a channel. It's a prayer. It's a source. And, like a lover, it comes when you honor it, make time for it, and cherish it. (Examining my past checkered relationships, I now know that these expressions may not guarantee that a love affair will last, but it definitely has no chance of lasting without them.) Without our expression, we would perish.

In honoring our creative expression, whether in art or business, we have the fortitude to face the unknown, brave new ground, and pioneer uncharted terrain. I prefer to view it as a continual balancing of the feminine and the masculine. Certainly we may dominate with one expression more overtly than another, but there is a constant pollination from within ourselves. The feminine whispers into our ear the inspiration and the call, while at the same time she nurtures us to confidence and brings the masculine to arms. The masculine initiates the action, the vision, and sets it forth into being. It's finding the symmetry, the perfect balance, of these two divergent sides of our nature (or our business's nature) and teaches them to work in harmony.

Naturally, I didn't know any of this when I first reported to work at Creative Artists Agency. All I knew was that I was excited. And scared. Very scared. It was the opportunity I had been working toward, and now that I had it, I was almost paralyzed with fear. I quickly realized that CAA was a high-wire act. One false step and my career could immediately plummet to the ground.

Ronnie Meyer was my safety net. He was also my friend, my angel, and my gift. Perhaps, most important, this powerhouse of an agent was my teacher, proving that George Bernard Shaw didn't know everything. It was from Ronnie that I learned how to really have courage, be emphatic and authentic, set goals, and run a company.

When I first met Ronnie, I was twenty-three and he was thirty-one. He was handsome, beguiling, and stood five feet eight on his toes. And in the early years he was always on his toes. It wasn't because he had any particular affinity for the ballet, but that he always seemed to be rushing somewhere. There would always be a deal that needed stitching together or a client whose fragile ego had to be massaged. And no one could squeeze more hours out of a day than Ronnie.

In Hollywood, "friendships" are often predicated on business, with its authentic and literal meaning drained from the word long ago. But everyone called Ronnie his or her friend—and meant it. Anyone lucky enough to know Ronnie had a friendship to cherish. His sense of humor was, and remains, wickedly sharp. The barbs were often self-deprecating, unless there was someone else around whose ballooned ego needed to be deflated. If they ever took offense at Ronnie's well-aimed poisoned darts, it was impossible to tell. They were always too busy laughing.

Ronnie was, to use his words about others he respected, "a stand-up guy." In a town where contracts are often the first step to a lawsuit, Ronnie's handshake meant something.

Ronnie had climbed the ladder the hard way. His mother was a Holocaust survivor; his father a traveling salesman who died young. In a rush to get on with his life (as I said before, Ronnie was always in a rush), he dropped out of high school and began to build a dream bigger than he felt he deserved. On this journey, fear took him a long way. Instead of allowing it to cripple him, he turned it into the fuel that kept him focused and continually striding toward his goal. His fear made it difficult to take him down. He made the most of every opportunity.

Ronnie's travels had made him tough. No matter how impressive the title and the office he would attain, inside he remained a rebellious punk who naturally bucked at the very sight of authority (ironic, really, when you consider that he often *was* the authority). If he ever flew off the handle at you, he'd make it a point to drop by your office later and apologize, muttering a contrite, "I'm sorry if I was tough on you." Then he'd immediately vanish, like he only half meant it. Still, I always appreciated the gesture, knowing that tantrums came easier to Ronnie than apologies.

When I arrived at CAA I had requested a literary traineeship. Having a mad passion for moviemaking, it was easy for me to visualize myself sitting with a screenwriter discussing his latest manuscript while he puffed on his pipe as he took in all my various ideas on how he could improve his intellectual tome. But these dreams never materialized, as I was very quickly plucked up and dropped at Ronnie's desk.

Along with all of his other talents, Ronnie had what is customarily referred to today as "street smarts." For a time he had been a clothing salesman and had honed the priceless knack of being able to read a person after only a few short minutes. It only took him those few short minutes to redirect the course of my life. Talking assuredly as if he knew me better than I knew myself, he told me that I had the personality of a talent agent. Taking this as a compliment, I assumed what he was saying was that I was good with people, although when I started working with actors, I wondered if he didn't just mean that I have a very high threshold for pain.

Ronnie trained me. Much like a puppy at imprint stage, I looked at his every move and studied him in detail. I knew I was learning from the best. Time and time again I'd watch him coax and cajole a star to go back to work. It could be a dangerous task, like dismantling a ticking bomb. But Ronnie did it with aplomb, making it appear as simple as tying a tie. (Perhaps simpler, as he refused to have anything to do with neckwear.) He'd have the matter resolved in a matter of minutes without scamming them, lying to them, or threatening them. His great ability was to make people feel seen, valued, and understood.

Ronnie's door was always open to anyone who needed

advice, words of encouragement, or simply had to rage in a
nonjudgmental direction. It seemed that everyone felt safe
pouring out their emotions to him. I got a glimpse into Ronnie's
thrall over the town when I was first assigned to his desk as a
trainee. Every year the Big Brothers of America would put on a
show-business bash, where Friar's Club comics would roast the
honoree until he was humorously blistered and charred. It was
a stag, all-men event, and Ronnie's popularity was so great
within the community that I would field fifty calls from those
who classified themselves as his "best friend" all wanting to sit
next to him.

Men weren't the only gender that reveled in Ronnie's company. Women adored being around him, and he certainly
returned the emotion. I understood his behavior well. Like my
own father, he was a delightful flirt. There are many powerful
men in the industry who don't truly like women and surely don't
understand them. They think of the opposite sex as nothing
more than the clichéd "notch on the belt." Ronnie's secret was
that he honestly enjoyed the company of women and cared
deeply about what made them tick. This proved to be a big plus
when it came to being an agent. Not every agent can pilot both
a female career and a male career with equal ability. Their strug-
gles are different, and it takes a sharp eye and a big heart to
understand and guide them through the various travails that
both sexes encounter. And Ronnie did it better than anyone.

When I was still a trainee, I accompanied Ronnie to "service"
Connie Stevens at a county fair singing engagement. CAA was

almost as new and as green as I was, although the primary color they were in was "the red." In an attempt to improve their current pigmentation, the guys had structured a deal with Regency Artists to represent their touring performers for television and film. We received a cut of their concerts; Regency, in turn, could bask in the security of knowing that their clients were being fully serviced in all areas. As Connie took the stage and started to perform, I sat back in my seat and began enjoying everything about the evening, quickly forgetting that I was there to do a job.

"Laurie, look at her," Ronnie suddenly whispered in my ear in his no-nonsense voice. "Look at what she's doing right now, because you're going to tell her after the show how much you appreciate her act. Pick out details so she'll know you really watched her." Ron was teaching me to be authentic. He wanted to make sure that whatever compliment I gave Connie came not only from my heart but from truly observing her essence.

I've never forgotten Ronnie's words, because the lesson he was imparting was too important, and not just within the narrow scope of the entertainment industry. The wisdom that he generously shared with me I have carried through life, clinging to it in both good times and bad. Here are a few guideposts Ronnie gave me on how to live life that I have taken to heart and made my own: Greet everyone with joy and interest. Be an answer. Be a friend. Do your homework. Be prepared. Push yourself to your greatest limit and only expect from someone else what you expect of yourself. If you're inside a conflict, talk to everyone and try to understand their point of view. Find a way to deliver bad news that allows them "to live to fight another day." As soon as you sign someone, you're terminal. If you've been hired, you will eventually be fired, so make it all count.

"It pains me to say 'no,'" he'd say. "Try to find a way to say 'yes.'" He felt that there were those who were smarter, more strategic, better tacticians, and who knew how to make a better deal; but he made sure he was the most accessible, that he'd call right back, which means right back. He was the best at letting other people know that they mattered.

He'd say work by some kind of consensus among the members in the department, so that the team is motivated to work for each client. Introduce people to each other; they'll probably create new projects. Put opposing forces in a room together; they'll usually find a way to like one another and remove the obstacle (but don't tell them that). If you are driven by money, you'll probably have a short career. Fear and insecurity drive everything. First identify the fear, and then manage it. There is enough to go around.

I listened and I learned, and Ronnie's wisdom informed the way I do business and, more important, the way I live my life. After a brilliant and admired career as one of the founders of CAA, Ronnie left. (His feet were always moving. It was only natural that he would follow them.)

Ronnie is now president and chief operating officer of that Hollywood behemoth, Universal Studios, still everyone's confidant and best friend. There's no doubt in my mind that had Ronnie been George Bernard Shaw's agent, that literary giant would have had to rethink his famous epigram.

Chapter Six

The Art of War

The art of war is like the art of the courtesan;
indeed, they might be called sisters,
since both are the slaves of desperation.

PIETRO ARETINO

IT WAS THE END OF 1976. America was celebrating its bicentennial and I was celebrating landing my new job at Creative Artists Agency (I'm only pointing out the coincidence and not making a comparison in importance). While women were transforming into an army of fierce competitors as they climbed the craggy escarpment of equality, I altered my wardrobe to fit neatly into CAA's narrow macho psyche. The irony was that I didn't feel at all self-conscious about following the limited, mannish dress code the agency had outlined for me. It seemed the request said more about them than it did about me.

I loathe admitting this, but the scarcity of women in the business when I first entered made for bitter jealousies among those of my sex. Although this might be a sweeping generalization, the word was that many of my sisterhood subscribed to tactics that were far worse than the ones used by men. They didn't stop at just maiming, but like any good predator went right for the jugular. That wasn't my style, and I promised myself it never would be. As best as I could, I would try never to succeed at the cost of my femininity. (I also made a pledge to myself that I wouldn't want to succeed based solely on my femininity.)

Offhand I can't imagine two men more different than Ronnie Meyer and Mike Ovitz. Mike may have been president, but Ronnie was the glue. Their lessons came from entirely different sides of the human spectrum. They were friends and partners in the same business in the same industry, but they saw the world from diametrically opposed points of view. As keen as Ronnie's intelligence was, when it came right down to it and a big decision had to be made, he would let his heart cast the deciding vote. The heart, as I quickly learned, was the one organ that Mike didn't believe had any place in the brutal world of deal-making.

Mike Ovitz was a student of Sun Tzu's *Art of War*. (You can learn a lot about a person by browsing through their bookshelf.) The first five essential elements are: Tao, Tien, Di, Chiang, and Fa (ethics, timing, geography, resource management, leadership, and execution). Out of nine elements, Tao—ethics—is always the first honored. Ethics is defined as the universal goodness that will always protect humanity as a whole away from a downward cycle.

Although Tao was number one on the list, it was Mike's greatest shortcoming. He had more of a "Do as I say, not as I do" philosophy when it came down to the nitty-gritty of running Creative Artists Agency. What Ovitz preached at the weekly meetings was for us to go out in groups, be a force, help each other network, and share information. It sounded very much like how you'd run a good government—or a good mob family. What he didn't say was that he subtly pitted each of us against the other, lending a strong, subliminal whiff of paranoia to the average workday. Mike was subversive, yet when he handed you your bonus, he'd shower you with praise in a way that had you walking out of his office feeling ten feet tall. And when you're that tall, you never think that you might be cut off at the knees the following day.

Mike was like Captain Ahab—unrelentingly driving his crew, pursuing his personal Moby Dick, blind to any possible disaster ahead, infecting his staff with his frenzy. Unlike Melville's one-legged madman, he was a master at galvanizing the troops, and his favorite keynote was that CAA was our company. He rallied everyone around the idea that their profit participation and bonus was, indeed, a representation of our piece of the rock.

That wasn't my motivating force. I wanted to rise quickly in my chosen profession. Before I was pregnant with my second child, I had climbed to the elevated position as one of the highest-earning agents in the business. Did I want to please Mike Ovitz and the rest of the boys? Very much. And even more than that, I wanted to impress them.

As with any endeavor, it's important to find out what our strengths are. As an agent I could parlay a good deal into a better one. I liked and admired "talent" and understood the pressures they were under, so I was always there to lend a sympathetic ear to my clients and their current woes. But my real knack, I found out, was to discover fresh talent. Company policy at CAA was to sign only those who had the potential to carry a project. Spotting the always-elusive "potential" is a gamble at best. All you really have to go on is gut instinct. But even as a novice, my gut instinct was still my most reliable chance for getting it right.

It was during 1981 that kids first started operating remote controls, which made them wrestle with quantum amounts of information at lightning speed. Music videos were the new fast-cutting, quick-moving art form that could be easily metabolized by the attention deficit disorder (ADD) age. The constant search for new talent wouldn't allow us to be restricted within the boundaries of our fifty states, and at that time England was revolutionizing advertising by adding commercials to the trailer heads of first-run motion pictures. British moviegoers sat captive to guerilla tactics designed to excite high-end consumerism. These weren't your run-of-the-mill television commercials slapped onto the big screen. Their budgets were larger, as was their imagination and creativity. The scope was specially formatted for the big screen, and to make sure they got the best, they hired full crews, solid writers, and directors who were resourceful and able to pack a dramatic wallop into a brief one to two minutes.

My friend, Leslie Morgan, had tipped me off that there was a hot new English director who was getting a lot of buzz on that side of the pond. She sent me his commercial reel. Halfway through my first viewing, I reacted as all agents must when they come across real talent, whether it is a director, a writer, or an actor: Without realizing it, you find yourself sitting up straighter in your chair, inching forward toward the screen, and suddenly viewing life a little differently. You're being allowed to see life through that artist's eyes.

The eye behind the lens belonged to a young man named Hugh Hudson. Hugh was in the middle of directing a film for producer David Putnam, and after watching his entire reel, I began to call Hugh regularly in an effort to sign him to CAA. Like a salesman on a mission, I took his reel around to each of my colleagues to make sure they were on board. (As I've said, the agents at CAA did their best work when they performed in harmony, and it was vital, when looking at a new potential client, that your associates know and admire his work when it came time to vote him in.)

When Hugh finally came to the United States, David Putnam set up screenings of their film for distribution sales. I brought Hugh into the office to meet everyone. Leslie and

Mark Rosenberg (then vice president of production at Warner Bros. Pictures) acted like a heavenly choir in singing my praises to the director, and Hugh signed with the agency.

The jungle drums beat very loudly in Hollywood, and word gets around quickly when something is noteworthy. Hugh Hudson's new film, *Chariots of Fire*, was more than worthy of all the talk it was getting. I naturally swelled with pride that I'd had the foresight to sign a virtually unknown director right before his career broke through. But as the proverb says, "pride cometh before a fall," and I went right down with it.

Mike Ovitz called me into his office and told me that I would no longer be the primary agent handling the skyrocketing career of Hugh Hudson. I'm sure he gave some explanation, but for the life of me I can't remember what it was. I probably didn't listen because I knew whatever he said didn't matter. The director was suddenly a very valuable client, and I wasn't considered an equally valuable agent to be navigating his next important steps through the obstacle course of the industry—especially when Mike was desperate to establish himself as the town's premier motion picture agent. Previously, Mike had made his mark in variety television, and he was murderously erasing that perception. Mike didn't put it that way, but in Hollywood nobody ever puts it the way they really mean it. It's up to the listener to extract the real meaning, which always seems to be soft-pedaled behind a toothy, understanding grin.

Certainly, I wasn't green. By 1981 I had four years under my belt, which is about twenty-eight years in dog terms—just about the same rate an agent ages. Mike poached my big catch for one simple reason—because he could. Owning the company wasn't enough; he wanted to build an empire. He more than got his wish. And if it meant stepping on toes, he didn't mind the crunch, especially when those toes worked for him.

It was a case of "What the Lord giveth, Mike Ovitz taketh away." And it was then that I realized my future wouldn't be determined by hard work but by one man's whim. That kind of insight doesn't give you a real sense of security. I was angry. I was bitter. I was hurt. And for that, Mike, I will always be grateful. I was forewarned.

Was I allowing Mike Ovitz to define me to myself? He lived his life according to *The Art of War*. Everything was either a victory or a defeat. Everyone he knew was either a friend or a foe. I knew that the only way to ever get his respect would be for me to take on the armor of his morality—and that I wouldn't do.

Without realizing it, had I handed over my entire belief system in myself to someone I neither liked nor admired? Self-love became my dogged aspiration; I would be the "me" my best instincts could ascend to. *Chariots of Fire* won the Oscar for best picture that year. Instinctively I knew I'd won something far more important.

Chapter Seven

Madonna

Is there anything in life so disenchanting as attainment?
ROBERT LOUIS STEVENSON

IN A SHORT AMOUNT OF TIME CAA had grown at an unprecedented rate, expanding like a guppy into a whale in both size and clout. For an agent still green behind the ears, it was exciting, fun, and glamorous. It was also like sitting on top of a polar ice cap just as global warming kicks in. Under those precarious circumstances, a wise agent went into his office every morning sniffing for the next superstar to be inked onto his roster.

Sometimes you just get lucky. Due to the arrangement CAA had with Regency Artists, I was assigned to represent the entire

Jackson family. It was 1979 and Michael Jackson had just cut *Off the Wall,* his big breakout album. Michael was polite, sweet, almost a wisp of a human being. Offstage his demeanor was still and hushed, as if he wanted to travel through this life without so much as rustling the leaves on trees. All of his many siblings were much the same way, and at first I thought they were the best-raised brood I had ever met.

Then I watched them around the family patriarch, the mighty Joe, and realized they were simply the best trained. I began to think of them less as a singing act and more like circus animals who sat on stools and did whatever the lion tamer holding the whip commanded.

Over the next few years I became close to the Jacksons' managers, Freddy DeMann and Ron Weisner. Like most managers their happiness was cemented to the momentary success of their clients, and at that time the Jacksons were riding a comet. Freddy took a liking to me, admiring my tenacity. I constantly brought him offers for Michael to star in big studio films. For probably good reasons, Michael would dutifully thumb through the scripts and then turn the offer down.

In 1984 CAA, that little agency that nobody thought had more than a wisp of a chance of succeeding, was devouring Hollywood in much the same way that Godzilla ate its way through Japan. Practically every big name in town was attaching itself to the agency, and I, who was too busy agenting to get around to my dream of becoming an ex-agent, was handling some of the hottest actors.

From age twenty-three to thirty-two, I was thought of by my colleagues as having a good "eye" for talent. I seemed to discover artists right at the moment they were about to explode. I saw "this special something" in everyone I signed. At the time I believed I was using "logic," but I'm sure there was a great deal of intuition involved. I'd look for a juxtaposition of two opposing forces, like they were sexy, but dangerous, or they were kind, but complicated.

There was an enigmatic pull toward their essence; in short, you could not take your eyes off them. Often I would pick a talent that had been an athlete or dancer, because at a base foundation they understood the amount of dedication and practice that went into an art. I studied the client list as a sample analysis of stardom. It seemed as though most of the clients, whether they were actors, writers, producers, or directors, were Jewish, Catholic, or African American—"minorities." I chose to believe that not only did they share a modicum of persecution and pain, but they enjoyed the antidote of ritual, comedy, and music.

CAA was also making deep inroads into music at that time, and although my plate was full, it was then that Freddy, displeased with the way that the William Morris Agency was representing one of his newer clients, offered her to me. It was Madonna.

Madonna's *Lucky Star* video had just been released, and getting dressed to go to work one morning I glimpsed the new video on MTV. Along with the rest of the world, I couldn't take my eyes off her. Trying to pinpoint the exact elements that make up a phenomenon is like trying to hang a cloud on the wall with thumbtacks. She was commanding; she oozed a steamy sensuality coated with a girlish excitement. But there was something else; something you could feel that was far too elusive to label. It was simply Madonna being Madonna.

I called my husband, Jack, over and pointed to the television screen. "Look," I said, sounding, I'm quite sure, like Sutter the moment he stumbled over his first gold nugget. "She's got it; she's this great contradiction of sex kitten and defiant rebel."

At that moment Jack was more interested in a food stain that had somehow landed on the tie he had wanted to wear that day, but, as always, he was supportive of any business decision I made. "Follow your instincts, Laurie," he replied, plucking another tie from the closet and swirling it around his neck. "You have great instincts."

I believe my intuition was one of the things Jack most admired about me—and most resented. He believed in it, but it scared him. I jumped on a plane and headed to the Hamptons to meet Madonna on the set of *Desperately Seeking Susan*. Trying to make a good first impression (CAA believed very much in good first impressions), I was decked out in a white mink coat and driven from my Manhattan hotel to my sandy destination in a stretch limo. This may sound glamorous, and it possibly could have been, but I was seven months pregnant with my second child and kept having to ask the driver to pull over whenever a sudden wave of nausea got the better of me.

We finally arrived at a beach of sand dunes that would

double for the Sahara Desert in the film. This usually serene area was at that moment bustling with activity, dotted with animal trainers, camels, trucks, actors, and crew. I stepped out of the limo weary and worn, as well as a very pale shade of green. I was met by Midge and Sarah, the producers and old friends, who, spotting my internal turmoil, immediately handed me a soothing cup of tea as they whisked me into their star's trailer.

Madonna's face and form have been seen and admired by almost everyone who lives on this planet. And yet, until you've seen her up close and personal, you've only glimpsed a pale imitation. The woman is nothing short of gorgeous, with luminescent skin wrapped tightly around a perfect frame. But it's the attitude that notches her into an alternate universe. Always and forever feminine, she has a sense of self and razor-sharp business acumen that would be the envy of every CEO. Before I could take my first sip of tea, she began to pummel me with tough but fair questions.

I respected her immediately. Here was a woman who knew precisely what she wanted and was more than happy to obliterate anything that got in her way. It was obvious to me that it wasn't simply her leadership that would turn this fledgling talent into a superstar and an icon. Madonna was the embodiment of the "New Woman," and I unconsciously identified with her need to succeed. Her sensual seductiveness and talent assured her survival, while she more than brought home her bacon.

When I asked her what she wanted, she did not tell me she wanted to be the world's greatest star. She simply said she

wanted to break down all the taboos. At the moment, I thought
she only meant taboos surrounding homosexuality and bisexu-
ality, but later I realized she meant all taboos. Madonna's mission was bigger than her own ego. Her crusade is to shine a
healthy light on the aspects of human behavior that society
would rather ignore. (In a somewhat ironic twist, she has helped
the world take off its corset while she put one on.)

Unlike many stars that paste on a persona, like it or not,
Madonna is her authentic self. The public can always spot a
phony, and their stay in the spotlight is usually mercifully brief.
Madonna's reign over pop music can only be matched by those
of Elvis and The Beatles. Instead of gluing her future to what
has already sold, she's had the courage to change her hair, her
clothes, and her music in whatever direction her artistic impulse
dictated. For one woman to stand alone on the musical mountaintop for that length of time is a towering achievement.

For me, Madonna was a rare example of someone who could
absorb all of her stardom and abundance without imploding
from her own success. Our meeting ended as most meetings
do: cordially, with a smile, and no decisions reached. I knew I
had passed the Madonna test, but I didn't know if she would
decide to become a CAA client.

The next night I was invited to a party that Diane von
Furstenberg was tossing for Barry Diller to celebrate his being
crowned president of production at Fox. Though I did my best
to act nonchalant, the New York show-business elite was not
my usual crowd, and I couldn't remember ever attending a party

by someone with "von" stuck in the middle of her name.

As I was standing on the buffet line, scrutinizing the various dishes and trying to find something that wouldn't kick off another wave of nausea, the woman standing next to me nodded toward the butternut squash and whispered, "Looks like baby food, doesn't it?" It took me a moment to realize that the attractive, conservatively dressed woman beside me was Madonna. She wasn't at all like the woman whose trailer I had been in the day before. The iron-willed sensuality and brass balls of determination had vanished, and now stood a woman slightly uncomfortable in her surroundings, just trying to quietly blend in.

Offstage, this icon was, in effect, just like me. I don't know why I was surprised. I had been around long enough by then to know that even the biggest stars, when taken out of their element, which they could create and control, were most often shy and uncomfortable. Madonna had created her own bubble of a world, and outside of that bubble she was nervous and less than sure-footed. Just like the rest of us.

We quickly bonded, as two people who find themselves uncomfortable in the same situation often do, and we chatted a good part of the night away. I can't remember anything either one of us said, but I assume it was meaningless and pleasant, which is always the key to good chatter. I know I enjoyed the evening and the companionship, and I soon learned that Madonna must have enjoyed it too. The next day I got a phone call from Freddy telling me that Madonna had decided to sign with CAA.

When I returned to Los Angeles, I immediately rushed to see Mike Ovitz, expecting him to catch some of my electric enthusiasm. With that monarch, enthusiasm is usually a one-way street. Mr. Ovitz has a number of varied abilities, but soothsaying is not among them.

Mike told me not to sign her. This wasn't a suggestion on his part. When Mike uttered anything he just assumed someone was in the back room chiseling it in stone. Obedience to his wishes was no longer my personal best. If I couldn't back my own instincts, then I had no right to be in the business. I'd lost respect for him long ago.

I called Freddy and told him that we were excited about taking on Madonna as a client. I was organizing internally and I would call him soon. Exactly what my next move would have been after hanging up the phone, I had no idea. Fortunately, I didn't have to find out, as fate decided to save me from the jaws of unemployment by sending me a wingless angel in the form of David Geffen. (Freddy had probably asked David to call Mike.)

Although David Geffen's name seeped into the public consciousness only after forming Dreamworks with his pals Steven Spielberg and Jeff Katzenberg, for years in Hollywood he was another king. He always seemed to me to be a great deal more comfortable with the power he wielded than Mike Ovitz, who appeared like a bodybuilder constantly flexing his muscles in a sad attempt to erase the ninety-eight-pound weakling he had once been from his mind.

So when David called Ovitz to rave about this incredible

new artist named Madonna, Mike actually listened. David had seen her cameo in the dailies of Harold Becker's new film *Vision Quest*. I was buzzed into the Ovitz office and told to set up a meeting with the "singer" immediately.

Naturally I was a few flights above elated, and yet I couldn't help but feel a little wounded that the same words I had uttered, coming from David Geffen had been met with such unvarnished enthusiasm. It was a lesson I would see repeated over and over again through the years. In Hollywood the messenger is often far more important than the message itself. The meeting took place in a small conference room, which probably only seemed small because of the number of people who were crowded into it.

Mike didn't believe there was any reason to have a battleship unless your big guns were visible, and for this meeting CAA was armed to the teeth. Besides Mike there was Ronnie Meyer, as head of the talent department; Tom Ross, head of the music department; Todd Smith, an agent who was on loan to Madonna at that time from Sean Penn; Freddy; and, of course, Madonna. But it wasn't the shy, reticent woman I'd spent the evening with at the party. This was business—her business—and she had morphed herself back into the juggernaut in charge.

All of us who are tethered to CAA sat up straight, as if we were afraid the teacher would rap our knuckles with a ruler if we dared to slump. Our good posture was no mere coincidence. Ovitz had rules for just about everything, and that included sitting, something I thought I was rather good at until he enlightened me. "Don't lean forward," he would constantly remind us. "You'll seem too desperate." Mike's posture, on the other hand, was his alone, and can best be called "remote." It seemed to perfectly fit his personality.

After greasing the conversational wheels with a few minutes of mindless Hollywood banter, Mike got down to the business at hand. "So, Madonna, you're this musical talent; what should we do if we get asked if you'll audition for a musical film?" he asked, a deliberate and calculated setup to see what she would do.

Madonna didn't answer for what seemed a little longer than eternity. She looked Mike square in the eye (something most people preferred to avoid) and then leaned in, placing a seductive shoulder and elbow on the table. Her long fingers began to play with strands of her blonde hair, dancing them slowly, sensually from one side of her ripe, pouting lips to the other, allowing them to languish erotically over her tongue.

As the lone female spectator watching this kittenish display, I was certain I was the only one in the room who could stand up at that particular moment without risking embarrassment.

"Do you know what I do when I get asked to audition?" Madonna finally replied, taking the hand that had been toying with her hair and aggressively turning it into a defiant gesture with middle finger up. "I flick them the bird."

We all broke out into gales of surprised laughter. All of us, that is, except for Mike. (Madonna wasn't challenging his manhood; she was just trying to experience it.) When the meeting was over, I walked down the hall alongside Mike, trying to get a sense of how he felt it had gone. It didn't take long.

"I don't want her," he defensively barked, with a wild display of scorn and anger.

Before I could try to counter his unexpected gush of venom, he continued. "Madonna, Cher, Prince, anyone with only one name, I don't trust them." I was tempted to ask him if that same rule of thumb went for Moses, but by then he had turned the corner and disappeared into his office.

As I tried to fortress all my arguments before confronting Mike, Lady Luck once again used the telephone to help me out. This time it was Mo Ostin, the president of Warner Bros. Records, who called Ovitz. He told Mike in passing that he was giving one of his new artists her own label, Sire, in gratitude for her releases exploding to the top of the charts. After concluding their phone call, Mike buzzed me on the office intercom. "Okay, sign her," he muttered before clicking off.

The next morning was CAA's big Friday meeting, where everyone announces what they're working on, jobs that are unfilled, and new clients that have just been signed. It's more or less the agency business version of comparing penis sizes. I never felt adequate in these meetings. I sat at the opposite end of the long table from Mike, appearing properly demure, while I could hear my heart drumming and feel the confetti being tossed wildly inside me. This was going to be my moment.

When it finally came my time to speak, I said, trying to sound professional and keeping my excitement in check, "I'm pleased to announce that we've just signed Madonna." Those few words were the summit of my career at Creative Artists Agency. It was all downhill from there.

With an anger and rage I'd not witnessed in the eight years I had worked there, Ovitz folded his hands into sledgehammers and pounded them on the granite table.

"See me in my office after the meeting," he growled.

After the meeting I didn't go running into Mike's office. I ran crying into Ronnie's office instead. Fortunately for me Ronnie had the best shoulders God had ever handed out to cry on. I was the worst kind of scared. I had no idea what I had done, so I had no idea how to prepare for the coming onslaught.

Ronnie did his best to console me without really telling me exactly what was going on. "Laurie," he said, sounding every bit the big brother. "Everyone knows all the work you put into Madonna." He was talking to me in agency code, and I understood what was happening immediately. Ovitz would take her from me. I should have seen it coming. He had done it before. Inside of Mike Ovitz lived a show-business tapeworm, always eating and always wanting more. In his mind the one-named Madonna may still have been less than family fare, but he quickly stopped being the morality police when it came to his profit. Her record had soared, her concert tours were guaranteed money in the vault, and "Like a Virgin" was on its way to making landmark history.

I always felt that Mike took his cue from Alexander the Great, who knelt down and cried when there were no more worlds to conquer. Mike, who viewed himself very much the conquering warrior, was determined not to run out of worlds, even if that meant he had to take those that he didn't really want.

I've no idea how Mike Ovitz spent that night, but I spent it crying. Countless nights during those years that I worked at CAA, I cried myself to sleep. Like many women during that time, I had allowed the job to blanket my life, at times throwing my priorities out of whack and short-sheeting all the things that really mattered. By now, I had tasted success, power, and money. And while Mike was eating his young and me, my infant son had pneumonia twice, my daughter cried the housekeeper's name before mine, and even I had to finally admit to myself that my marriage was on its last legs, and those legs weren't going anywhere anymore.

I watched Madonna's career skyrocket from a distance. That bitter pill became my—and my children's—greatest gift.

Because one morning as I looked at myself in the mirror and applied mascara to my bloodshot eyes, it suddenly flashed through me: Like coming out of the woods at dusk to see the inviting smoke billowing from the chimney of a friend's house, I remembered that my objective had never been to be an agent. My goal was always to become an ex-agent.

And with that I was free.

Chapter Eight

The Best Laid Plans . . .

There is a tide in the affairs of men . . .

WILLIAM SHAKESPEARE

I CLOSED THE DOOR TO Creative Artists Agency and that chapter of my life in 1985. I had entered that embryonic company as a neophyte. When I walked away, it had grown into a Hollywood powerhouse, and I was now a married woman with two children, having schemed and dreamed with many great talents in the business.

I admit that I cried when I left the dysfunctional home that had taught me everything I knew about the inner workings of the industry. But I didn't cry as much as when I worked there. That's always a good sign.

I was finally going out into the real world (at least as real as Hollywood can be) to become a producer and work for myself. I could make my own hours and be there more for my family. Over the last few years my marriage had become a well-ordered shambles inside a very polished outer shell, perfect viewing for friends and family alike. Jack and I both grabbed the only thing we could hold on to: our work. Like many in a similar situation, I hoped that success in that arena would somehow radiate into all other areas of my life.

Jack had an overpowering personality coupled with an extraordinary ability to continue talking long after any other mammal would have to stop to catch a breath. This is great in an agent but not quite so wonderful in a husband. He made me feel as if I was second in command, and second in command in a marriage isn't in command of anything.

I come from a long line of women who complained about the men in their lives. They expected, and demanded, that their mates protect, provide, and defend. Anyone short of Lancelot was bound to be in for a lot of grief and bitching, and even he would probably end up wanting to spend more time at the Round Table than at home.

I accused Jack of being angry and anxious, not realizing that in this one way we were the same, although we handled it differently. He could explode better than me, while I was superior when it came to quietly fuming. Although we didn't give personalities letters back then, I was definitely a type A, A+ if you graded on the curve. In short, I was the mirror image of everything I resented in Jack, and now neither one of us was proud of the view we were seeing anymore.

One of the reasons I had fallen in love with Jack was because we seemed to have so much in common. Our likes, goals, and ambitions all seemed pointed toward the same distant bull's-eye. But now as we were making great strides toward that destination, the cracks in our relationship were beginning to show, even though we both tried to ignore them. Since the days when etchings were first being doodled on cave walls, it was a matter of survival of the fittest and each gender had their definite role to play.

In these gender-blurred times we can only hope that we safeguard against doing each other in. So why, then, do we try? Especially with a belief in life after life, is competition even necessary? Maybe only as a motivation and nothing else? It's a way to keep score. *But to keep score of what?* (At least I was pondering.)

My husband's personality quirks, which I had thought were endearing at the inception of our relationship, now made me run for cover. His sense of humor laced with dark irony, which had once had me doubled over in laughter, had become a few shades blacker, and it all seemed rooted in fear. He was used to showing his love of family through worry; now he perseverated in a parade of horrors that would doom us all to catastrophic result. When we were just starting out, I would sit in awed silence listening to a man I considered a brilliant raconteur; now it seemed he never shut up, repeating himself so often I could finish his sentences just by watching the way his lips moved. At the beginning of our relationship I admired his abundance of passion that made it almost impossible for him to sit still. Now I watched him pace like a trapped animal, and as his wife, it would be my job to throw out the unmendable socks that he had worn holes through.

How much Jack had actually changed and how much of the change was mine, I couldn't really say. But I am sure that love is the most potent of mind-altering drugs, and when that's drained from a person's system, we are left feeling angry and alone, betrayed by life's cold realities. In my heart I knew my marriage was beyond salvaging. Maybe if I were not struggling in every area of my life, maybe buoyed by some cinematic success, my relationship with Jack might somehow spark with a renewed energy and exuberance. If this sounds naive, as indeed it was, it was because I wasn't thinking; I was hoping. And hope has a way of trumping all other emotions when necessary.

The tearing apart of our marriage had been coming for a long time, but we did our best to allow it to continue to grind on. As the cliché goes, two people either grow together or they grow apart. The spirituality I kept secret started to deepen. I began going to intuitives for readings, throwing runes and casting the I Ching, trying to use external props to make a divine connection. The only problem is, when you're doing it in the name of true love, the guidance realm can't help but be amused, and they'll give you disinformation, scrambling your signal until you have no choice but to dig inside to find that most elusive love of self. I felt compartmentalized and conflicted. Jack's world remained rooted to the more basic five senses. We were no longer two young and obscure agents fighting for a foothold within the industry, and it seemed that now the only things we had in common were our children.

Unfortunately, ending a bad relationship is much like knowing when to put a sick pet to sleep; we always allow it to drag on longer and more painfully than it should. And so, by mutual, silent agreement, following in the grand tradition of marriages that have curdled over time, we settled for being married strangers—at least until the hollowness finally became too much to bear.

As our marriage sputtered toward its natural and foregone conclusion, I pinned the blame on Jack for not applauding my spiritual exploration, although now I see he simply remained the same man I had married. I was the one busy splashing around in uncharted waters trying to make sense of what I thought would make me happiest. Nothing seemed to fit.

Perhaps I should have been more understanding of his cool and concrete view of the world and not expected his participation in trying to peek outside its tactile limitations. But love is the most demanding and unreasonable of emotions, and every slight from our partner wounds like a slash from a saber.

It's been two decades since Jack and I both picked up a pen and signed our names to the divorce papers. Without love overheating our passions and fueling our resentments, I have found my ex-husband to be a good and true friend. The things we used to fight over are still the same things we can't agree on today, but with love out of the equation, it no longer seems to matter. Simple friendship permits both parties a freedom of thought not allowed or tolerated in relationships where cleaving is involved. But this awareness came to me only after the fact, as knowledge always does. Unfortunately, wisdom is the caboose on the train of life.

I allowed the wreckage of my marriage to limp along like an elephant looking for the nearest burial ground as I took all my energy and poured it into my children and my new producing career. Soon after leaving CAA, I made an overall producing deal with Warner Bros. I considered this something of a coup, as very few lone female producers had their own production companies back then. An overall deal is coveted by everyone in Hollywood—and regretted shortly thereafter.

A studio, whether it's Paramount, Fox, or Warner's, gives you money, an office on the lot, a parking space, a telephone, and an expense account. In fact, they give you practically everything but the green light to make the movies they've hired you to make. The luxury and the frustration are both overwhelming, like making love nonstop for years without ever reaching an orgasm.

But I was lucky. I had a rabbi. In Hollywood parlance, the term "rabbi" has nothing to do with religious beliefs and everything to do with finding a mentor in business who will expend time believing in you and will help you create the future you envision for yourself in your dreams. When I set up my tent at Warner's, I had a rabbi and dear friend in Mark Rosenberg, who

READER/CUSTOMER CARE SURVEY

We care about your opinions! Please take a moment to fill out our online Reader Survey at **http://survey.hcibooks.com.**
As a **"THANK YOU"** you will receive a **VALUABLE INSTANT COUPON** towards future book purchases
as well as a **SPECIAL GIFT** available only online! Or, you may mail this card back to us.

(PLEASE PRINT IN ALL CAPS)

First Name _____ MI. _____ Last Name _____

Address _____

State _____ Zip _____ City _____

Email _____

1. Gender
☐ Female   ☐ Male

2. Age
☐ 8 or younger
☐ 9-12   ☐ 13-16
☐ 17-20   ☐ 21-30
☐ 31+

3. Did you receive this book as a gift?
☐ Yes   ☐ No

4. Annual Household Income
☐ under $25,000
☐ $25,000 - $34,999
☐ $35,000 - $49,999
☐ $50,000 - $74,999
☐ over $75,000

5. What are the ages of the children living in your house?
☐ 0 - 14   ☐ 15+

6. Marital Status
☐ Single
☐ Married
☐ Divorced
☐ Widowed

7. How did you find out about the book?
(please choose one)
☐ Recommendation
☐ Store Display
☐ Online
☐ Catalog/Mailing
☐ Interview/Review

8. Where do you usually buy books?
(please choose one)
☐ Bookstore
☐ Online
☐ Book Club/Mail Order
☐ Price Club (Sam's Club, Costco's, etc.)
☐ Retail Store (Target, Wal-Mart, etc.)

9. What subject do you enjoy reading about the most?
(please choose one)
☐ Parenting/Family
☐ Relationships
☐ Recovery/Addictions
☐ Health/Nutrition
☐ Christianity
☐ Spirituality/Inspiration
☐ Business Self-help
☐ Women's Issues
☐ Sports

10. What attracts you most to a book?
(please choose one)
☐ Title
☐ Cover Design
☐ Author
☐ Content

FOLD HERE

Comments

was then sitting atop the studio as president of production.

Unlike many perched in that powerful position, Mark was warm, smart, and nurturing, with an easygoing nature that drew people into his orbit. Dinner at his house was an event, filled with gossip and laughter and the most succulent lamb chops that ever graced a plate. Not surprising, as Mark would dash around town before having friends over to pluck the choicest meat he could find from numerous butcher shops. It was his habit to scrutinize a lamb chop with the same scrupulous eye he used on screenplays and dailies.

Unfortunately, when it came to taking care of himself, he wasn't quite so fastidious.

Mark was eighty pounds overweight on a good day. He smoked and drank, both to wonderful excess, getting immense pleasure out of all the vices that are looked at disapprovingly by those with stethoscopes and X-ray machines. He was afflicted with the usual set of accompanying diseases, diabetes and hypertension, and yet he never allowed it to cast a pall over his attitude or how he chose to live each day.

Mark's passion was making movies. Movies that said something either political or deeply human. He believed celluloid should be more than just sprockets stringing together car chases and explosions. After a failed marriage to Lauren Shuler, who added the hyphen and "Donner" to her name after she married the director Richard, Mark came full circle and finally wed his long-ago love, Paula Weinstein, then an independent producer. Mark met Paula back in their radical days when they wanted to overthrow the establishment before discovering they could make a damn fine living out of it.

For a brief moment in the California sun, they were a golden couple sitting on top of the world. But as every child with a globe can tell you, the world is constantly turning. I don't know if Mark realized just how limited his time on earth would be, but he was surely savvy enough to understand that his present position at the studio came with a very short shelf life.

In the days of Louis Mayer and Darryl Zanuck, these men were ensconced on their plush studio thrones for decades, secure in their positions, without fear that the slight movement of a decimal point in the bottom line would create industry panic and cost them their jobs. It's a different ball game today, and anyone who takes that lofty position at a studio knows before-hand that he is stepping onto the conveyor belt to oblivion.

I had never thought of the studio without Mark, although the warning bells began ringing shortly after my arrival. The most important producers on the lot at that time were Peter Guber and Jon Peters, who had bestowed upon a waiting world *The Color Purple, Flashdance, Batman*, and *Rain Man*, giving the duo heavy-duty clout to spare.

Rumblings around the lot whispered that the mighty pair had already chosen Mark's successor, their handpicked prodigy, Mark Canton. Mark Rosenberg's ear was always planted firmly on the ground, so he, no doubt, heard these rumors as well. I can only imagine how difficult it was for him to show up at Guber's house that sunny afternoon where they were throwing an engagement party for Canton and his bride-to-be, Wendy Finerman.

Along with the usual chitchat and clinking of ice were the sidelong glances my friend Mark could feel even when his back was turned. He brushed it off like lint from his shoulders and continued to carry himself with his customary aplomb, until he carried himself too close to the pool, took a misstep, and fell in. When he hit the water, he knew his Warner Bros. career was over. We all knew it at that moment. I didn't know what to do other than watch in horror. King Lear didn't have a sadder fade-out.

It was seven years after that plunge when Mark Rosenberg died suddenly of a heart attack at the age of forty-four. Whether his body called it quits due to overindulgence or disillusionment I can't say. I do know that he was particularly susceptible to a heart attack, as his heart was already broken.

Only five years older than I was, Mark was the first colleague and dear friend I had lost to the other side. The passing of anyone you love is painfully difficult to deal with, but when it's one of your own troops, it feels as if a piece of yourself has been amputated. The night before Mark's funeral, I curled up in bed, cocooned in my comforter that was of very little comfort. I was finally slowing down and allowing myself all the natural emotions that come with loss.

Then, seemingly for no apparent reason, I could feel the hairs on the back of my neck begin to bristle and the charge of electrical energy suddenly surround me. And I could hear Mark's voice inside me. I was channeling my dear friend. And although an electrical field seemed to encase me, I felt a stillness of tranquility that seemed as if it was radiating from within. I could hear Mark's voice, but it was more than that. I could feel his voice, the texture of his thoughts. He said quite simply, "I'm with you." My rabbi, my friend, lovingly came to me. The extra electrical field helped show that my belief system was indeed true. He gave me the strength to take on popular resistance. The activist he was pushed me physically. He knew I needed more confidence. Mark told me to keep going.

When a consciousness dies, it may choose to operate from the same thematic purpose of expression. Mark had been my truth seeker on this side. His guidance wasn't about to end because we now existed on different planes. He was to be my aide-de-camp to help me unlock the other side. Channeling is thought to exist in the realm of the mystical when it's not deemed downright nutty. Eyelids are prone to flutter while chairs suddenly begin to dance across the room. It is usually considered more fitting for a magic show than a belief system, as ripe for parody as politicians and deodorant commercials. It's an almost impossible concept for many to wrap their minds around, and I don't understand why.

AARP conducted a poll in June 2007, "three-quarters (73%) of respondents 50+ agreed strongly or somewhat with the statement 'I believe in life after death.' Women are more likely to believe in the afterlife (80%) compared to men (64%)."

Both *Time* and *Newsweek* have run multiple cover stories about prayer in relation to healing, and continually point out that as a nation we are strong in our conviction in God and the existence of angels. So why have we dismissed our intuition and not realized its worth? It very possibly might be the unheard voice of a loved one on the other side, be it God, Jesus, saints, Mohamed, Buddha, sages, ancestors, and friends.

Remember, there are senders and receivers. The first step to asking for help from a higher consciousness is to invite contact. Prayer, reflection, and introspection may ignite the invitation. Consciousness has the ability to send us messages when we give permission. The signs, however, may be subtle at first. Listen for cues or be open to unexpected sources. You may have a body knowing, a gut feeling, a waft of energy; and then be on the lookout for resonance from a lyric, a dream, a photograph, etc.

The permission is given by our soul, our God-self, our elevated consciousness that guides our lives. The other side also needs permission to hear our thoughts. Our ideas are our own. So be clear about what you want, stay tuned to your God-self, and love each moment.

Chapter Nine

Frances

A teacher affects eternity; he can never tell
where his influence stops.

HENRY ADAMS

EVERYONE IS A TEACHER.

This odyssey that I've been on has taken me from classroom to classroom with sharpened pencils and newly bought spiral notebooks, but the truly wonderful teachers whom I've learned from haven't been professional educators, but friends and mentors who showered me with their affection, beliefs, and philosophy.

Perhaps the greatest of these guiding hearts was a woman named Frances. I first met Frances when Jack and I were only recently divorced. He had quickly gotten back on the horse and became engaged while I was still emotionally in the stable. I was dealing with the mess that our marriage had made for our children.

I spent an inordinate amount of time feeling sorry for myself, even though I didn't know who that "self" was anymore. I was no longer a wife, a full-time mother, or a theatrical agent. I had been stripped of all the external essentials that used to help reflect my world back to me. I felt like a forgotten ghost ship lost in the fog.

Self-pity can balloon to immeasurable proportions during the holidays, when loneliness seems to dog every thought and action. Thanksgiving was the holiday my heart most dreaded. All the customary warmth and food and family had been pulled out from under me when Jack decided to take the children on vacation with his new fiancée and her children. They were all going merrily off to bond. I acted the part of the good sport, at least until the front door closed behind them. I was left alone and devastated.

As Fate would have it, and Fate always has her way, that Thursday I was plucked from wallowing in my own silent despair by a welcome call from Magda, Jack's mother. She was a remarkable woman, all warmth without judgment and one of the blessings that Jack had brought me that I had promised myself I'd hold on to even after the marriage ended. Fortunately, she felt the same way about me and was calling to invite me to Thanksgiving dinner at the house of her stepson, Brian.

It was there that I met Frances, Brian's mother. Usually at holiday get-togethers, people are introduced, chatter and laugh, have an immediate kinship, then forget one another's names before the tryptophan from the turkey wears off. It was different with Frances. We quickly burrowed through the small talk and were soon discussing metaphysics between bites of chestnut dressing and cranberry sauce.

And for the first time in a long time I didn't feel quite so strange and alone. Frances understood my emotional state all too well. She had felt strange and alone most of her sixty-plus years. She was born in 1927 in Boston, a time when that city was severely straitlaced and took enormous pride in the phrase "Banned in Boston."

Frances's mother had been a brilliant college graduate (rare for a woman at that time) who studied both physics and math. Her father was a prominent physician of upper-class Boston. Her first mistake in her parents' eyes was being born a girl. They had both wanted a boy so much they had only bothered to think up a male name for their heir, and when Frances was born, both surprising and disappointing them with her unexpected gender, they only bothered to change one letter, then quickly gave her the manly nickname of "Frankie."

Frances was an only child and exceptionally smart. Instead of reveling in his little girl's intelligence, her father would verbally abuse her on a regular basis. Both parents constantly tormented Frances by telling her to "shut up—no one wants to hear from you." At a very early age Frances began to retreat inside herself, spending days in silence and cold isolation with no touching.

By the time she was eight, when other girls were busy jumping rope or toying with their mother's makeup, Frances had rounded up the neighborhood children and started a math tutorial in her house. When the mother of one of Frances's students called to complain that her child's numerical skills were not improving, Frances's mother actually berated her eight-year-old for her inferior teaching ability.

When she was nine, Frances contracted polio, distorting and twisting a body that she had already begun losing contact with because of her parents' abhorrence to physical touching. (She had been predicted to grow to be five feet seven inches, but the bend in her back only allowed her to reach the height of five feet two inches.)

Frances suffered through the long, painful stretches of loneliness in silence, finding it all but impossible to make human contact. This finally led the little girl to begin communicating in what she called "the subtle realm." Rather than contacting those living through the "earth plane," Frances began making the connection on the "etheric plane." Over time her contacts would be from those who had already passed on. She began to predict events and outcomes, and fine-tune her psychic ability.

When interacting with other human beings, Frances could be coldly aloof and flinty. The polio had left its mark, not only on her body but on her personality as well. The curvature of her spine transformed her into an object of ridicule. The constant jeering from the children echoed her father's derisive voice. Her body had become a walking representation of the tired refrain that had followed her since birth.

The disease and the accompanying pounding silence acted like a buzz saw on young Frances, separating her mind and body. Her mind would "take off," finding a small oasis of solace in her convoluted internal world. This escape from self served as the only railing she could prop herself up on with any consistency. Like a wound in the process of healing, her awake world and her fantasy world fused. Her sense of self depended greatly on the detailed messages she constructed in her thoughts.

Over time the subtle realm of her spiritual world became, for Frances, her one and only environment for truly loving expression. It was there that she wanted to have contact with others. It was only there where her distorted frame wasn't the first thing noticed by wide eyes. It was safe. There were no bodies that could touch. There was no defiled physical form that she had to outstretch with an abject fear of rejection. It was the only world left to Frances where she felt she could truly be herself.

Still, in many ways Frances struggled against her inner self and attempted to somehow fit within the narrow parameters of that era's prevailing "American Dream." As in any Judy Garland–Mickey Rooney movie of that time period, Frances married the boy next door (which she claimed was "told" to her at the age of twelve). She would stare out her window, waiting patiently until Alfred came home, then spring from her house and launch into a lively conversation.

Following the fairy-tale template, he became a doctor and they had two children, and all should have been right with the world. But nothing was ever right about the real world that Frances inhabited. Although she exhibited unusual self-control over her explosive personality when dealing with her son, Brian, she was fiercely critical of both her husband and daughter.

Frances was a brilliant woman. If intelligence were all that was needed for change, she most certainly wouldn't have repeated the identical mistakes her parents had made while raising her. Unfortunately, a necessary component in altering behavior is the ability and desire to see life through someone else's eyes, as well as their emotions, and Frances couldn't do this. She truly believed that she possessed the only viewpoint that mattered. This was my teacher's great weakness, and the one that would eventually swallow her life.

After seventeen storm-filled years, Frances and her husband divorced. She had very few friends and a myriad of hang-ups, especially concerning sex, which wasn't hard to understand and sympathize with, since her own physicality was something she had spent years trying to escape from. In an effort to "open herself up" Frances participated in therapy workshops and explored sex, and though this led to a series of male encounters, she never lived with a man again. Alone now, Frances spent much of her time in the ethereal, bristling more and more whenever the tangible world intruded. Her daughter naturally rebelled against her mother's dictatorial ways, leading to a break in their relationship where mother and child didn't speak for two years.

Frances kept only one friend at a time. Each friend was required to devote constant and perennial pledges of allegiance to her reality. Her ability to allow others to compete or disagree was exaggeratedly low. Being her "friend," if that word is even applicable, was a kind of enslavement. If you weren't completely on her side, she felt rejected. Any relationship with Frances quickly began to feel like a tightening noose. Naturally, under the circumstances, her ability to hold a friendship was excessively short. Frances believed most people had toxic energy fields, and, indeed, her relationships did become toxic, ending with her "friend" escaping to get some needed fresh air. Each one was quickly forgotten, as easily tossed aside as prizes plucked from a box of Cracker Jacks.

A sense of humor can often keep even the most ardent of zealots from giving in to their excesses. Frances was blessed with a keen wit, and would often use it to help someone else keep the balance in their lives. (Whenever I would start to overindulge in a mad dash to better myself, she would respond by saying, "You could die from improvement.") Sadly, the wit and wisdom that she could aim in someone else's direction when necessary had little effect on the way she conducted her own life.

After that Thanksgiving, with the strong gravitational pull of her personality and her beliefs, I was immediately drawn into her inner circle. (As I've said, she usually had only one friend at a time, so I was all she really needed to complete her circle.) Frances studied and taught astrology at UCLA. She channeled energy and practiced psychic attunement. Frances taught me "bilocation," the ability to be in two places at the same time. She believed that the precursor to that work had been her ability to communicate "in the subtle." Frances was convinced that if "all" was energy, that if we were simply energy, then certainly we could defy our location of it.

Although I never dared mention it, she had been looking for an escape from her small, twisted body since she was a child. I saw myself in her, yet I loved the world. I began to meet with Frances at her house, along with two other "seekers," Kim and Sandy, almost every day for sessions that could last up to four hours. Those times provided some of the most intense moments of my life, where Frances gave me a refined spiritual language, and I, in turn, offered my study and experiences about life after life.

If she positioned herself in the lofty role of teacher, she was superior, above, and still not truly connected with another. It was through her mind, used as a psychic tool, that she could finally reach out to others, speak to others, feel into others, and finally connect. It was there, in the subtle, that she found the only antidote to her pain.

For Frances the isolation was ameliorated with great psychic attunement. A controlled environment mitigated her fear. It was only when she had to come down from her perch and mingle with others as an equal that Frances felt truly lost. Because of Frances, I began to understand how important love of self and others at the same time would become.

Her body, which she always thought of as her enemy, never stopped betraying her. By the time she was sixty-five, Frances had undergone two mastectomies. Although she was being eaten away from the inside out, Frances was convinced that she could alter the cellular division of her cancer. She believed that if she had truly forgiven her parents for all their abuse, her body should have ceased the physical annihilation of the cancer. Yet, with all of her devout dedication of psychological, physiological, and metaphysical work, her body was still grounded in the here and now of flesh and blood. Her failure to turn her teachings into a slashing saber to fight against her disease left Frances angry and completely confounded at how all of her work with energy could not be applied now to her withering, septic body. I believed in what she was trying to do, I just knew that she was going about it from anger.

One day while all four of us were channeling together, tapping into Universal energies to guide us, Frances asked Kim, Sandy, and me how long she had to live. She had just received her second cancer diagnosis and, as we know, recurrence is terrifying to say the least. Both Kim and Sandy believed she could "process" herself into spontaneous remission. Remember, will and belief are the mightiest of elixirs. I had the arduous task of stating my truth, "You have two years." Frances banished me from the group. I understood. Even if my vision was true, and it ended up to be so, why would she want that sentence hanging over her head and have the person who handed down the sentence in her inner circle?

That being said, if we are capable of accepting our inevitable death, either literally or symbolically, we become less attached to the outcome. We become better intuitives and keenly aware of signs transmitted to us by our higher selves. We come to the realization that our physical body is truly a gift from which to learn our own unique sequential order on this earth plane. Our life cycle is more than simply we are born, we live, we grow older, we die. It's in the actual passing through our lives in a physical body that we come to understand why the order in which things happen matters. The profound gift of the physical is to experience our personal evolution before we return to the realm of the non-physical, the ALL, where we can then apply what we've learned—an education which could only be attained in the physical realm.

Indeed, we may be able to come into fleeting resolution with the split, the conflict, of the part of our soul that wants to reconnect to the ALL versus the body consciousness fighting for survival through sovereignty. The conflict between one and oneness has confounded human beings for eons. "Oneness" defies the beliefs and physics we collude to share about our material world, yet is the perfection of symbiosis of creation and the ALL.

The lucky ones among us, before they pass over, try to make peace with others as well as themselves. All the vital things that life has offered us that we've managed to overlook or eschew are suddenly viewed with crystal clarity. Life's treasures that we never had time for or were deemed too petty seem to spread out before us, and it's up to us to take our last moments while on this earth to appreciate them.

Frances could not do this. As she died, she remained brittle and unforgiving. With her last breaths she still preferred the "subtle," not believing that people are truly in their hearts. This was how Frances, in her solitary world of two cats, two friends, and two children, held herself together as she died. Was Frances my teacher? Definitely. Was she my friend? After all these years, I'm still not sure.

True friendship is based on a mutual feeling of equality and a desire to help that other person become all they want to be and not all you want them to be. If that definition was applied to my friendship with Frances, then Frances was definitely not my friend. She simply wasn't capable of adjusting her emotions to allow any other individual to stand on the same footing where her ego was planted.

I have also come to a conclusion that I refused to admit to myself when my great mentor was still alive: Frances was crazy. I'm not trying to be flippant, and I've selected that word only after careful consideration. A traditionalist might have diagnosed her as "schizotypal." This isn't to say that I didn't learn greatly from her, or that I don't agree with many of her beliefs and philosophies. But by choosing to live her life more and more on the "etheric plane," Frances had dislodged herself from reality, and therefore, humanity.

Unlike Frances, I love this world and this body, and I love people. I didn't take on her life; I took the tools. Believing in life after life doesn't mean we can toss away our presence in the here and now as if it doesn't matter. It all matters. Life is a living, breathing, tactile gift, not to be squandered simply because our consciousness extends beyond the borders of our own flesh.

That, I'm sad to say, is one truth my dear mentor never understood.

Chapter Ten

Full Circle

The character and history of each child
may be a new and poetic experience
to the parent, if he will let it.

MARGARET FULLER

IT WAS 1993, AND I WAS TEETERING on the cusp of forty. It's a difficult age for a woman, both physically and emotionally, and a number I'd vote to have eliminated from a female's aging process the way elevators in buildings skip the thirteenth floor.

Overnight, it seems, the music we listen to is suddenly relegated to oldies stations, and we're told matter-of-factly by doctors that our eggs are rapidly turning to dust. Spider veins pop up out of nowhere, and our rear ends drop a little closer to the ground every time we stand up. We need glasses to read, and what we had thought of as "laugh lines" aren't so funny anymore. Still, forty does have its compensations. It's also the age when many women stop to reevaluate their lives and examine the choices they've made along the way—and perhaps even try to correct a few.

With children of her own now in tow, it's natural for a woman to take the time to assess her own relationship with her mother. Often, it is a Pandora's box of pain, regret, and condemnation, and there are certainly times you kick yourself for ever having pried open the damned thing in the first place. But you can't clean it out if you don't open it first.

I certainly wasn't the first daughter whose rocky relationship with her mother was in a constant state of flux. There is something inherently frustrating about being a daughter, just as there is with being a mother. The way Nature has it set up—I wish I could think of a more delicate way of putting it—is that as one begins to bloom the other starts the process of wilting. The sadly parallel arcs of life are, for some, a petri dish for jealousy. The daughter yearns for her mother's freedom of maturity while the mother longs for thighs without cellulite and some snappy ovaries.

Years can go by and circumstances drastically alter, still some mother-daughter relationships often remain frozen in a time long ago. Between skirmishes and battles, mothers and daughters constantly scratch at the door of understanding, but seldom push it open wide enough to build a bridge. It's as if we're too busy bristling over bygone hurts and distant wounds to really talk and to really hear.

As I approached forty, I was determined that, for the first time, my mother would really hear what I had to say. As it turned out, I was at just the right age to rearrange the landscape of my emotions. There had been seismic shifts in my world, and I was definitely losing my footing on ground I could no longer be sure of.

Only a short time earlier, my future had seemed carved in stone. What I hadn't taken into account was that stones sink. In the blink of an eye, my marriage was over and my mothering was not beyond reproach. Much had gone wrong in my life, with so many holes punched into the "master plan" I had designed for myself that now I felt I had to make something right.

It's as if mother and daughter spend those precious formative years creating their own little dance and stick to those rigid steps long after the music of parenting and childhood has stopped. Finding myself suddenly dead center in what is charitably referred to as "middle age," I desperately wanted to change the choreography between my mother and me. I had tried many times over the years, but the hint of confrontation sent my mother into defensive posturing. So that's where our relationship stayed, unspooling like a private movie in my head, until I had at long last garnered the necessary tools of knowledge and courage.

I had come to realize that spiritual growth is the pathway to what we all yearn for and yet continually deny ourselves: inner peace. That's the true promised land we're all desperately searching for. And if we're ever to reach it, we must be willing and free enough to crack open our belief system to allow the spiritual to help us, soothe us, and guide us to value life.

Certain changes we can make only in small increments. It doesn't matter. Simply, through the very process, we learn to know ourselves well enough to instinctively feel when we're ready to take the next step. And isn't truly knowing ourselves really the heart of all change? Back then I believed that nothing worthwhile ever came easily. (Perhaps this is why so many lottery winners end up being miserable once they cash those giant checks.) I thought it was the work to get there that was as fulfilling as the eventual destination, and the victory we feel within ourselves for finally reaching it that we ultimately cherish.

And now I finally had to put myself to the test. All guidance was urging me. I was determined to confront my mother. Naturally, I had already tried. I'd spent years intermittently trying, but I would walk away rebuffed and cowed, my heart heavier than before. Try taking on an alcoholic. When I became an adult, my relationship with my mother was polite. Too polite. For fear of opening up an old war wound, we paid only minor lip service to the thin umbilical cord that still connected us, keeping our weekly Sunday phone calls short and inconsequential.

When my own daughter, Jessica, was twelve, I felt an indefinable pull to see my own mother and hear her say just four words to me: "I am so sorry." There are just some words we all have to hear before we can at last free our lives to move forward in a healthy direction.

I didn't want her to feel any guilt. That wasn't my intention. My goal was for both of us to finally, at long last, purge all that bile we had painfully layered over our relationship those many years and have mutual forgiveness. I didn't know what her reaction would be, and the fireworks this could possibly set off scared me. Still, once I decided that a true relationship for us was impossible without those words being uttered and breaking down the wall that separated us, I flew from Los Angeles to Miami, where my mother still lived, to confront her.

For accuracy's sake, I must correct the above impression of heroics on my part. At the last moment, fear took control of me and I almost backed out, but my mentor Frances wouldn't allow it. She knew this was the time, but didn't tell me why. In a few days, I would learn the reason for myself.

I brought Jessica along so that in later years, when she needed to confront me, we would both have the courage and the freedom to take each other on. I had made up my mind that when she reached the age of forty, she wouldn't have the same relationship with me that I had had with my mother. I had to break the cycle.

The first day we were there was filled with shallow pleasantries and innocuous small talk. It was the usual treadmill of banality my mother and I walked together whenever we wanted to have what we thought of as a "good visit." I'm sure I told myself that I was just waiting for the right moment to confront her, although there never is a "right moment" for that sort of thing. All you can really do is to find the least "wrong moment" and then go ahead and do it.

It was the next day, when I finally seemed to run out of excuses for putting what I was there for on hold, that my mother and I sat alone in the den to confront our past. I told her there would be no blame, no recriminations, no verbal assaults aimed at a distant memory. What I needed was for my mother to hear my pain, with the hope that this wouldn't just be an emotional cleansing for me but for both of us. The wounds that had been living inside me came tumbling out, and my mother, who had chopped off similar attempts of mine for a moment such as this by reacting with both fire and ice, listened quietly. For the first time, she truly listened.

When I finished, finding myself both exhausted and exhilarated, I asked her to say those most difficult of simple words, "I am so sorry." She didn't even have to mean them. She just had to say them, like an actor reading her lines, or better yet, like a friend who was saddened by a friend's pain. I had to hear them.

Was I being childish? Perhaps. But I was, after all, her child, and in that most difficult of relationships, the rules are whatever works. The emotional umbilical cord can never really be cut. What I wanted, what I needed, more than anything was to finally untwist it from around our hearts so that we could love each other freely.

My mother looked at me for a long moment, and her eyes,

which could scare me so as a child, suddenly began to mist. "I am so sorry," my mother said. But it was not an act, and she broke down in tears. As you know, I had only seen her cry once before, and that was when her mother died. Needless to say, my eyes welled up, and my tears seemed enough to fill an ocean. As gut-wrenchingly emotional as that moment was, crying never felt so good.

The next day when I entered the kitchen, my mother was doing the dishes. I noticed that she was having trouble standing, and after a little prodding, she admitted she now had difficulty writing. She told me she would be going to the doctor for tests on Monday. But in her heart, I believe, she already knew what they would say.

Five years earlier she'd had breast cancer, and most likely it had returned, navigating a deadly path to her lungs and brain. We fell into each other's arms and held on. Crying never hurt so much. And right then I knew why Frances had insisted that I didn't dare delay this visit with my mother. Time, that most misused of God's gifts, was suddenly at a premium.

For so long I had wanted to be honest with my mother about all my pain. Still, I never would have confronted her had I known that she was sick. Completing the circle, she never would have granted herself the permission to have been so open with me had she not felt that her time here on earth was soon coming to an end. It was the perfect moment, perhaps the only moment, where the two of us could meet and grasp on to all we really meant to each other but had never been able to express before then. The mother I had always needed was in my life for the first time.

There is a moment in almost every parent/child relationship when the weight of strength and guidance shifts from one to the other, as if we were straddling some sort of seesaw of life. It's the time every child has to grow up whether we want to or not. After my mom received the diagnosis that she had expected, I decided it was important, for both of us, to give her the greatest gift you can give a grandparent: the time to really get to know your grandchildren.

Decades ago, families (especially Jewish families) remained within close proximity in a particular neighborhood, growing up together and growing old together. Uncles, cousins, and aunts all made for one large, single entity. Families are now splintered all across the country, connected only through e-mail, phone calls, and the occasional family reunion. They say the world has gotten smaller, and maybe that's true, but the distance between loved ones has become achingly large. And so it wasn't unusual that every time my mother saw my children they were no longer the children who had kissed her good-bye on the last visit, with no resemblance to the framed pictures of them she kept on her nightstand.

I made an oath to myself that my mother was going to have a real relationship with her grandchildren, and I immediately began taking my two offspring, Jessica and Aaron, to Miami at least once a month. As stern and as hard as she had been to me while I was growing up, she now did a complete about-face and was loving and soft to the grandchildren she adored but only now was beginning to truly know.

My mother again went through her debilitating courses of chemo, and they added Gamma Knife surgeries, which seemed to do its medical magic, at least temporarily. Six weeks after she finished her last chemo treatment, the cancer had returned—the tumors were back. And the eventual outcome was clear. It was then that I decided to share with my mom my spiritual beliefs concerning life and death.

As my personal convictions grew and developed over the years, I was careful not to sprinkle them in my parents' direction. I was not afraid that they would turn my entire belief system into a source of humor and derision; it was worse. I was afraid they wouldn't hear me. After all, ridicule requires attention.

As my mother faced her death, an outpouring of all the borrowed wisdom of Elisabeth Kübler-Ross and Kenneth Ring's, *Lessons from the Light*, as well as what my own journey had taught me, came rushing forward. I was so swept up in my own fervor that only somewhere in the middle did I become self-aware and nervous. It struck me that never before had I shared with her what mattered to me most, and now her reaction was one I had never received from her: acceptance.

I was finally able to give my mother the comfort and peace she had never been able to attain before. I began flooding her with books to read. I told her about my meetings with those who had flatlined and been brought back. I spoke of my work with Frances. And, most important, I taught her that there are senders and receivers and that intuition is often our gift from the guidance realm.

"Remember, Mom, how you taught me that the soul is eternal? Well, it is."

With death pulling her farther and farther away from this earthly plane each day, she seemed to hold tight to all I had to say. And the more we talked, the more I could see the soothing glint of inner peace filling her ever-widening eyes.

She was vulnerable. I was vulnerable. All of the defenses we had both surrounded ourselves with over the decades dissolved, and every moment became invested with the sharp, serrated sorrow of why, when we'd just finally found each other, did it have to be over?

Yet this time together was also sweeter and richer and deeper than it had ever been before. She would look at me with that look that can come only from a parent when she finally takes in her child. There's that utter amazement when she wrestles with her own insignificance and realizes she created this wondrous being. Now we had the connection that I'd always longed for.

Over the next few months I watched my mother grow weaker, but at the same time grow stronger in the beliefs that we were beginning to share. As her eyes became sunken and hollow, a speck of what I can only call divine light seemed to dance almost softly in her eyes. It was as if her soul was finishing its packing and was at last getting ready to move on.

Aaron's tenth birthday was in June 1994. I asked him if he wanted to go to Miami to celebrate it. My children and I boarded a plane for Florida, consciously knowing that this might very well be the last time they would ever see their grandmother. From somewhere inside herself my mother ordered up the strength to take the children to dinner and play cards with them on the floor. But it wasn't long before whatever stamina she had somehow managed to muster finally gave out.

In September I got the phone call we all dread. I was told that my mother only had a few days left to live. I immediately jumped on a plane and went straight to the hospital. Viral pneumonia complicated with cancer cut down her oxygen supply, putting her in a delirious state. She kept attempting to get out of bed, her spinning mind convincing her that there was a conspiracy of stealing in the ward, which agitated her. She was uncomfortable, and those who loved her most suddenly became the enemy.

I told my father that I wanted to sleep with her that night. I worried that with her discomfort she would pull out her IV. Finally, after a dose of heavy antibiotics, my mother came out of her delirium. By this time, when my father, my brother, and I were in conference with the doctors, my mother was furious that she wasn't included. After all, it was her life and she wanted to be in charge. She went on a rampage, and she accused my father of only wanting to get on with his life.

She said to me, "You have no idea, Laurie, how selfish your father is."

I can only imagine how those words cut through my father's breaking heart. For the forty-seven years my parents had been married, my mother had been the structure. My father may have been the one who brought home the money, but she was the one who had substantiated their entire existence. Where they lived, how they lived, with whom they lived—this was all my mother's purview. My father had relinquished the reins of their future to this woman, and in doing so, she became his complete world. My mother had friends. My father's only friend was my mother. She was the giver; he was the receiver. She was the one in control. Always.

And now my father was suddenly thrust into the role of care-taker and decision maker. The world my parents had created was now his to attend to, and he had to attempt to hold it together for as long as possible before it crumbled in his hands. He had to arrange for hospice. He had to arrange for a wheel-chair. He had to arrange for food to be catered in. He had to arrange to take her home.

"You have no idea, Laurie, how selfish your father is," my mother had said cuttingly.

Certainly he had been, once. But no more. Her dying helped my father become a giving, caring, diligent head of the house-hold. This growth would prove to be his salvation in finding himself.

Except for the occasional outburst brought on by drugs and the vicelike tension of the situation, I was able to quietly observe how much my father really did love my mother. With my mother's death now almost tangible, they finally came together without the fighting, the put-downs, the bickering, and the barbs that had come to define their relationship. With the time they had left now so suddenly short, they didn't waste a moment of it in diffused states of inebriation, beneath a fog of pills, or in constant contention. It was then that my father rallied the best of himself to show my mother just how much he truly loved her. He began to express himself with a greater dimension of connection and truth than ever before.

As she withered away from her disease, he was passionate in telling her how beautiful she was. "Gerry!" he'd say, "you're as beautiful today as the first day I laid eyes on you." By this time she had lost all of her hair, and most of her body weight, and couldn't stand up, so, of course, she didn't believe him. At least not at first. But when she saw the way he looked at her when he said it, she believed that he believed.

Watching their bond of deep devotion as my parents' relationship drifted through its final stage, I pledged to find the kind of love that didn't have to be on the brink of death or in dire circumstances to force a depth of connection, but a love without defense—a love that was appreciative of every moment and didn't take time or itself for granted.

I was starkly aware that my definition of love eliminated sparks, infidelity, conflict, and pain. A tall order, perhaps, but love is an emotion, defined and molded only by the two people in love. At this point in my life, I was learning about what love could be from my parents—remarkable!

That day we had a meeting with my mother's oncologist and neurosurgeon, who came to the joint conclusion that there wasn't much else that they could do. That night, my father, my brother, and I gathered around my mother in her room. She had a difficult time concentrating, and when she could form cohesive thoughts, she had trouble speaking.

These are always the times when a family tends to think it best to wrap the truth in cotton, feeding false hope to the one who's dying like it was a placebo. I broke through the usual platitudes filling the room when I finally said, "Mom, I've flown in because we need to talk about your death."

This may sound like a harsh dose of reality to say to a dying woman, but my mother and I had discussed death for months, and the subject was like an old friend. A moment after I said it, my mother became laser sharp. She focused, centered herself, and looked at me with unbending clarity.

"Mom, we have very little time," I told her. "But what time we have, we want to talk. We love you very, very, very much and we're here to be with you through it all. We want you to know that we believe in the other side, and that we'll be with you forever. Just because you might be dropping your physical self doesn't mean that we won't be communicating."

And then it happened—and I still get goose flesh when I think about it. Although by this point my mother had little muscle control or the ability to speak, she almost seemed to momentarily usurp our strength, and she very definitely and clearly said, "I promise we will communicate, and I promise we will always love each other forever."

We were all immediately awash in tears. My brother left the

room, went to his meeting with his support group, and told them that he'd seen a miracle.

We all had.

When I slept in the hospital room with my mother that night, she told me that she wasn't afraid to die. Looking into her eyes, I could tell that these weren't hollow words of courage on her part. Our long talks about life after life had erased any and all fears she'd had of stepping over to the other side. Her thoughts were of her three grandchildren, and all she could ask of life now was for them to grow up to be strong, healthy, and sufficiently happy.

The following day the usual parade of doctors marched to my mother's bedside. She was very weak and could barely talk, but once again she forced herself to focus and somehow managed to pull herself into a state to be able to speak to each one of them. It was an exhibition of sheer, undiluted willpower that I have never seen equaled.

Very slowly, very arduously, very deliberately, she asked them if there was any other place to go, if there was any other clinic to call, if there was any other procedure to be done. She asked them if there was any chance that she could and would ever have her life back.

Some of the doctors replied tenderly, while others answered her query in a cold, medicinal manner. But from whatever direction their answers came, the destination was always the same. They offered no promise, saying that anything that they could do wouldn't bring a return of any noticeable significance.

After having what she already knew in her heart underlined by experts, my mother went to sleep and didn't awaken for two days. She'd had internal cerebral bleeding, and when her eyes finally did snap open, she couldn't speak or get up without help. But, mercifully, she had no pain. And the following nights I slept with her, watching her and studying the wondrous transformation that had taken place inside my mother. There was a quiet grace to the woman now, and where there had once been thorny agitation was an inner calm. My mother was finally attaining the soothing tranquility she had always longed for in life.

Before the cancer, my mother talked incessantly. Attempting to participate in a conversation with her could be grueling work, and you were often relegated to the role of audience while she slammed home whatever points she was trying to make. With all those words firing in your direction, it was easy to not really recognize how loving she was. The words somehow got in the way. After all, sound is filler. It relieves us of the burden to be connected to the other person. The one prattling on can go into their own head and not really have to reveal who they are. As for those pretending to listen, as long as their gaze appears attentive, they're free to let their minds wander as far from the unceasing monologue currently assaulting their ears as possible.

Throughout my mother's entire life she was always one step ahead of herself. She was perpetually anxious, busily planning dinner during breakfast, mentally hopping to the dry cleaner while on the way to the grocery store. In retrospect, it seems that my mother spent the whole of her lifetime dashing. And it was our job to dash right along behind her. We never questioned, because my mother was in charge. Now her soul was in charge.

The uncanny timing began a transformation that was a gift on many levels. She was extremely happy. She was full of life. There was a real delight inside her that I'd never seen before. She never abdicated her personality, even though now she didn't speak. She made noises, she rolled her eyes, and she cupped her hands to the right or to the left to pretend that she was whispering and in mischievous cahoots with me against the nurse. And all the while she was laughing. There was a sense of serenity as well as joy in her eyes.

It was as if Nature had stripped her to the barest of essentials, and we were, at last, allowed to love her for what she really was—for what she had always been but we, and she, could not see. Now her eyes would light up when we walked into the room. All she wanted to do was hold our hands, stroke our hair, and touch our faces. When my mother lost her voice and that route of communication was suddenly gone, people willingly opened their hearts just trying to connect with her. The loving was so pure.

My mother and my brother had had their silent wars while he was growing up. Theirs remained an enmeshed relationship of codependents. All the warmth and affection that she withheld from my father, she gave freely to my brother. He, in turn, kept his feelings frozen in the fetal position. That was the

emotional blackmail that kept him from rebelling and in tow
. . . until he walked into the hospital room alone one day. Summoning up whatever strength remained in her, my mother again spoke, with a revived conviction and clarity that I can only assume she summoned from the gods: "Bruce, I'm sorry for everything I have ever done." These were the last words my mother would utter until the moment of her death. My brother wept. With time quickly running out, they finally had their chance for mutual forgiveness. And all the pain and blame were immediately lifted from their hearts.

On his morning rounds the next day, the doctor was stunned to see my mother sitting up in a wheelchair. This rag doll of a patient was actually getting stronger. He knew it was only a temporary ray of hope, but he felt we should take full advantage of it. He believed she should go home and, with the help of hospice, have her journey be as comfortable as possible.

We, too, understood that the eventual outcome hadn't changed. But just because a miracle may have a short shelf life doesn't make it any less of a miracle. Now that my mother was stronger and happier, I took this time to run back to California and resume the life I had been neglecting and was now in sorry need of repairing. I would call my mother every day, and though she couldn't speak, I would fill her in on all the good things that were happening in my life and the lives of her grandchildren. Even though she couldn't vocally volley with me, I could feel her newly buoyant spirit bubbling on the other end of the line. And as I talked, I would close my eyes and visualize that spirit in the strong, healthy body that had once been hers. That spirit and that body together: that was the mother I had always wished I had grown up with.

One week quickly blended into the next. My father would report to me that my mother would have blackouts, but then she'd get up and have something to eat, as if nothing had happened. She could barely feed herself. She had no inhibition, she had no modesty, and she had no vanity, like she had before. The disease had returned her to the childlike state of "just being." Now she had only purity and an openness to love. She was starting her journey into the other realm while she was still here on earth.

Frances had a gut knowing that my mother would pass that weekend. She was only confirming what my own heart and intuition were telling me. I needed to be by my mother's side. Now.

When I arrived in Miami late that Thursday, my mother was sleeping. My father, with his scotch, and I, with my tea, spent the night sitting in the living room, drinking and talking. And talking. My dad told me how very afraid he was. Yet, in stark contrast with his emotions, he looked so much better than the last time I'd seen him. There was solidity about him, and he seemed so much more in the present than I could ever remember. Having my mother in that house, having to take care of her and love her and give to her, made him so much fuller. It brought out the quintessential essence of his character, and now he truly was much more of a man.

When my mother saw me that morning, she was elated. She smiled, cooed, gently stroked my hair, and tried to speak. The sounds were whispered and garbled, but I listened. I listened and laughed and responded because it was my mother's way of connecting, and whether I understood the words or not didn't matter. I could read everything that was in her heart just from her eyes. It was her last hurrah.

My father watched this playful interplay I had with my mother, telling me later that he was struck by how different she was with me now than how she'd seemed over the last few days. All she had been doing, he said, was sleeping. Those snippets of time when she was awake were dotted with blackouts. He couldn't believe her now lively expression or sudden increase in energy level.

My mother and I spent most of the day together communicating with mangled words and tender touches, and then it was suddenly evening. I wanted to be by her side when she died. And, in truth, I didn't. Very simply, I was scared. As much as I believed in life after life, I didn't want that hand I was now holding to go cold.

Before I left Los Angeles, I had asked Frances's son, Brian, the medical doctor in our family, to tell me what being around death was like. His reply took a moment as he searched for exactly the right words that would encapsulate that particular overwhelming emotion. Finally, he told me that often it was a "mystical experience."

The next morning, my mother blacked out in my arms, and I wasn't afraid. I felt that it was a harbinger of things to come. And as I held her limp frame close to mine, I knew I had just stepped through a big portal. In our old dynamic, my mother and I were in disconnect. She didn't let me in that close, as if there was a force field around her that couldn't be penetrated. And if she played the one in control, then by default I was the one who was out of control. It made me feel helpless to be around her postured strength, and I eventually found it best for my own survival to stay away from her. It was exhausting circling her orbit, which forced me to rebel in search of my own structure. Until the end.

My brother was going through a similar metamorphosis. He had always allowed our mother to be his structure, like my father had. It was just easier to hand over his will and his destiny to this woman than to enter into a fight that he knew beforehand he'd lose. He had also suffered from a learning disability. He never went through the healthy rebellion that teenagers do to help them establish the most fitting path for them to take in life.

Only when our mother got sick did my brother allow himself to blossom into his true character. He began to stand on his own, finding and decorating his own apartment, starting a new dental practice, divorcing his wife, and working his way into a new and fruitful relationship with his son. It was no mere coincidence that all of my brother's accomplishments happened at precisely the same time my mother was diagnosed with terminal cancer.

The weight of my mother's personality had been too much for my father, my brother, and me. But mostly, it had been too much for her. Too many of life's barnacles had attached themselves to her psyche, and her emotions cast a shadow over our every step. And now the weight and the shadow were suddenly lifted from all of us. As she stood precariously on the welcome mat outside death's door, my mother could at last relax and be her truest self. And, in turn, so could we.

My mother would boast that her children were her greatest accomplishments. She had married at sixteen, given birth to my brother at eighteen, and then had me when she was twenty-two. When she turned the corner of fifty, my mother, reflecting on her life (unaware of the full import of this succinct summation), said, "Just when you've experienced all that life has to offer, along comes a grandchild."

She was blessed with two packages from me and one from my brother. She loved being a grandmother and had a knack for it that she hadn't had for mothering. When she was well, each visit was a party of balloons, toys, special foods, merry-go-rounds, ice-skating, or Disney World. As I watched her life ebbing away, I was warmed by the thought that if grandchildren were, to her, the last gift that life had to offer, then now at sixty-three, her life had been complete.

Sitting by my mother's bed, tenderly stroking her motionless hand, we both knew that our parting would only be temporary. For most of our lives my mother and I found it difficult to really talk. Now we had made a promise to speak to each other after she passed. She would advise me, help me, and guide me. She would do all the things that I had needed her to do all along.

We take it for granted that wisdom and love are infused into every soul the instant it passes over. There is no reason for us to assume that these attributes attach themselves to a spirit simply because the body it lived in has died.

For most of her life my mother had been critical, tyrannical, and argumentative. In death, she would have to work to remove all of this earthly armor she had accumulated, finding the best essence of herself. As much as we have to change to reach out to them, those on the other side must also be willing to go through similar changes to reach out to us.

It was 5:30 PM when Alberta, the nurse, came into the living room and gently told my father and me that my mother was dying. I asked her how she knew. She looked at me with a wisp of a smile, and in a tone as comforting as warm maple syrup, she replied, "Mrs. Perlman came out of her coma to say, 'Home, home, I want to go home.'"

We immediately called the hospice nurse, who, after arriving and seeing my mother, told us that she barely had a pulse and would most likely die within two hours. I quickly called my brother, who came right over. We all gathered around my mother. My brother was to her right, whispering in her ear what a great mother she'd been, and then he knelt to recite the "Serenity Prayer." I stood at the head of the bed, caressing her brow. And my father was to her left, holding her hand gently, as I imagined he did when they were sweethearts.

My mother, in her last hours on this earth, looked like a baby—no hair and toothpick frail. As I stroked her brow I thought, *She birthed me into this life, and now I am birthing her from this realm to the next.* Her entire body was stiff; only the faintest pulse still beat under the paper-thin skin, covering the hollow where the neck and collarbone meet. Under my hands, I felt all the energy from inside her body suddenly rush to her head, and she was blanketed with a thick electrical field. It was much like when you touch a television and can feel the static electricity.

Her soul was that electrical field. It had left her body and was hovering; I could feel it. My mother now came to be my true inspiration. I could see how much peace my belief system had given her, and now my mother was physically substantiating all of my beliefs.

The medical experts had predicted that my mother would be dead within two hours, but at seven the next morning, this woman still clung to life by the thinnest of invisible threads. I couldn't understand why. I knew from our conversations she was no longer afraid to die, and we had all, at long last, made our peace. Still, she wasn't quite ready to cross over. Not yet.

By eight the next morning the hospice rabbi made an unsolicited call to check in on my mother. Told that she was dying, he immediately rushed over. At 9:10 I took him in to see her. I walked to her right, the rabbi to her left, while my father stood in the threshold of the door; we all watched as she took her final breath.

Then I knew why she had valiantly hung on until that precise moment to pass over. She had waited so the rabbi could take her home. She had waited so her funeral would be on the day of my parents' forty-seventh wedding anniversary.

Until the very end, my mother was in charge.

If my mother, at an elevated consciousness level, a "soul level," was this much in charge of her death, then we are all that much in charge of our own lives. Because of my mother's death, I had finally found my calling. I made a silent pledge to myself to bring spirituality to psychology from the devout belief in life after death.

My mother made good on her promise and became my most significant guide.

Chapter Eleven

Divorce, Hollywood-Style

*The only solid and lasting peace
between a man and his wife is,
doubtless, a separation.*

LORD CHESTERFIELD

IT'S IMPOSSIBLE TO PINPOINT EXACTLY when a good marriage stops being good, but like pornography, you know it when you see it. The first blush of romance brings to the fore the best of our childlike instincts. We become more playful, more inquisitive, and more carefree. The world is transformed into a big sandbox, and simply being alive is a holiday. It also has the additional side effect of making one myopic, and it's impossible to see how something so wonderful could ever go wrong.

Love is romance after it grows up. It's certainly deeper and richer and wider in scope. It's also work. In the feathery bubble of romance, nothing seems to matter. When it develops into love, everything seems to matter.

Marriage is the next logical step (although even the great poets have never been able to figure out what's logical about love). Love can quickly lose the playfulness that was inherent in romance under the weight of mortgages, diapers, leftovers, and overdrawn checking accounts.

Quite simply, romance is the unexpected delight of a flickering firefly, while love is a light bulb that constantly needs changing.

Before we were married, Jack and I had a wonderful romance: warm, tender, passionate, with a feeling of being just naughty enough to keep our libidos ever vigilant. Whether true or not, it felt as if we didn't have a care in the world. Then we were married and had two children— along with all the accompanying responsibilities that go along with wedded bliss—and suddenly there was a great deal to care about. And if our relationship lost some of its earlier high-kicking energy, as a couple we became more intertwined than ever before.

The obvious question (I know it's obvious because I've asked it of myself a thousand times) is "What happened?" In the vast majority of cases, I don't believe that any one thing can end a marriage. It may have been Brutus's knife that finally felled Caesar, but there had been a lot of stab wounds leading up to it.

With Jack and me, the always handy "irreconcilable differences" seems to cover it. It was really a process of slow erosion, as when the lip of the ocean laps away at a sand castle. As a couple, we appeared to have everything, and maybe we did. It just wasn't the everything we wanted. People do grow apart, and over time they can change radically, until their former selves are little more than a distant memory. If one doesn't constantly build new bridges to their mate's changing interests, eventually there's nothing left connecting them.

As I've said, Jack's dream had been to become a film director, so being an agent for directors became the bitter pill he had to swallow every time his phone rang and a client living the career he had always envisioned for himself was on the other end. Success is the sharpest of two-edged swords, and nothing can compensate for it, if it's that other edge you've always desired most.

Although I took my work seriously, perhaps too seriously, my career had managed to lose a lot of its luster. I started to feel like a butcher who slowly begins to realize there's more to life than just pork chops. As I did as a child, I began to spend more and more time alone in the bedroom, seeking the solace within myself that I couldn't find anywhere else. I began to meditate at an altar I had placed in our bedroom. Jack, as was his custom whenever he was confronted with things spiritual, made fun of me. But I didn't care anymore.

With all Jack and I had in common, we were becoming like two trains on opposite tracks heading in different directions. Jack would only consider going to God as a last resort, while for me, going to God was the first line of defense. And that became an ever-widening cavern between us.

Whenever I would underscore events as beyond coincidence and nothing short of divine design, Jack would quickly and derisively end the conversation by quoting Sigmund Freud's famous line, "Sometimes a cigar is just a cigar." (Personally I've always felt Freud chose to believe this because, himself being a cigar smoker, he didn't want to have to question his own masculinity every time he lit up.)

When he was a little boy, Jack said good-bye to his uncle Sidney at the airport. He cried because he had a feeling that he would never see his favorite uncle again—and he never did. Sidney died of a sudden heart attack. "Knowings" scare him. And even today, Jack still hides under the covers.

I was, and remain, his direct opposite. When I was told that my girlfriend's aunt had just passed, it was natural for me to open up the avenue of connection to the other realm, and I dropped my head into my hands and silently prayed, *Dear Aunt Hanna, please watch over Joyce and Carly* . . . And then, as if on cue (as metaphysically I believe it was), a musical button on my counter that played the song "New York, New York" went off without having been pressed. There was no "short" in that button, and it had never randomly gone off before and hasn't since. There was no possible way that button, without being pressed, would have gone off at exactly that precise moment.

I knew instinctively that this was Aunt Hanna's way of reaching out to me, acknowledging my request. The guidance realm is omniscient and communicates often as an electromagnetic field, such as buzzing in the ears, a sudden electrical chill where the short body hairs stand up, lights going on and off, mental messages, and so on.

Often our personal guidance realm is made up of our ancestors working silently to network on our behalf. Inviting your guides to come forward and make themselves known is as simple as a silent prayer. Leave room for the possibility that your guides have worked on themselves since their earthly expression. Often they have found self-love and are able to serve you graciously. In your invitation for them to come forward, demand that they show up in love and light, and on your terms.

I don't look for signs where they don't exist, but I believe it's just as foolish to ignore them when they're there. In my research I've found that this is often a common occurrence when someone who has died wants to catch our attention and break through to us, but we so often want to put it down as a mere coincidence. It seems that many people, like Jack, just don't want the hairs on the back of their neck standing up. In that case, the guidance realm colludes to stay hidden for a purpose.

It may be true that opposites attract, but as Jack and I became more and more opposite, the marriage began to grind to a halt. My proclivities, which had become so important to me, were like nails on a blackboard to him. In a fruitless attempt to keep our marriage afloat, I was forced to put a large part of me in a box and nail it shut. Obviously, hiding such a significant part of my nature was doomed to fail, and so, too, was the marriage.

When I left the womblike warmth of the studio system to become an independent producer, I felt alone and lost in the darkest, densest part of the forest. I found myself frozen with panic, not sure which way to turn. A few years earlier I would have been able to turn to Jack for guidance, strength, and comfort. Jack now responded to me as if I were another of his troubled, inconvenient clients. But at the time I needed him most, our marriage was in tatters, and my husband was no longer emotionally available to me.

It seems that while I was in our bedroom meditating, I thought he was off having an affair. He denied it, of course, but all the signs were there, lit up in neon. Naturally I wanted to believe him, but by now I had devoted my heart to always seeking the truth, and this particular truth was too obvious to miss. I imagine I could have gone on a feminine rampage, like a wild boar that had just been wounded, but I chose not to. In my own mind I certainly didn't condone his libidinous sideline, but I most definitely understood it.

You see, I too had a secret.

Jack and I had gone into marriage counseling, where the trite and the mundane that had built up over the years were picked at like old scabs, causing very little upward change in our relationship. I think we both realized we were beating a dead horse, but we were both so inert inside the corral we had created that neither of us could move.

Instead of dealing with the reality of the situation, my mind nestled into a fantasy life my imagination had woven for me to play in. I had what can only be described as a fixation or crush on Michael Keaton. When I first saw Michael, I was still an agent. He was bouncing as a guest star from one sitcom to another, considered by many to be an always reliable utility player but not much more. By chance I saw him on *The Tony Randall Show*, and I could tell immediately that he had the magic—it was too obvious to miss.

Michael was performing his stand-up routine at the Improv, and I went to see it, double-checking my first reaction to make sure that everything that lit up in my memory really did exist. He knocked my socks off. I glanced around at the audience to see if their reaction was the same as mine. As I suspected, by the time he finished his act, there was no one in the packed house whose socks were still on their feet.

I started drumbeating Michael's name to every agent at CAA. The agency was now only interested in signing talent that could star in a film, and Michael Keaton at that time was just a bit player. I had to walk into each agent's office and insist they watch ten minutes of his guest appearance. I wouldn't leave their office until I hoped they saw what I saw.

Eventually the other agents joined me in launching Michael's fledgling career and giving it a big push. The agent, Michael Menchel, landed him the juicy part in *Night Shift*, and my husband, Jack, followed up by bringing him the lead in *Mr. Mom*. His résumé had suddenly turned to platinum, and I was able to make him an overall deal at Fox.

But not just any deal. In Hollywood it was nothing short of

groundbreaking, surpassing the deals that had established heavyweights like Eddie Murphy at Paramount and Clint Eastwood at Warner's. I was immensely proud of spotting Michael Keaton's talent and lifting it to the cinematic heights where it so obviously deserved to shine.

But it wasn't all business. I melted a little every time I was around him, and I allowed myself to melt considerably more in my thoughts, where no professional barrier kept us apart.

Show business has always been sexually charged, where the intermingling of ideas often leads to nectar of a more sensuous variety. I was more than capable of acting coquettish, but it was always in the spirit of fun. I tried to never get close to the deep line I had drawn separating the personal and the professional.

But that line becomes difficult to detect through eyes blurred with tears. (Not that I showed up with anything less than a game face.) Michael and I had a relaxed, easy rapport dotted with continuous laughter, like two kids playing hooky. He was as funny and charming in life as he was on the screen, with a genuine shyness that made his naturally boyish quality even more endearing.

I represented him through great success for ten years. When I became a film producer, my marriage was in its last gasp. Still, I couldn't help but feel guilty about my innocent, fantasy attraction. I so wanted my marriage to work, and I had been working hard to make that happen with the most meager of results. Now what I really wanted to do was play, but only safely in my head. Knowing the dangerous waters my heart was entering, I never ever wanted to reveal my secret conjurings.

Michael and I were in New York on separate business and had slated one night to see a Broadway show. Punctuality is almost a disease with me, so I arrived early and knocked on his hotel room door. He opened the door, dressed beautifully for a New York evening, except he hadn't yet put on his shoes. I noticed this made him just a slight bit shorter, and brought his eyes that much closer to mine.

I sat down as he walked across the room and began to squeeze into his shoes. Then he said, with an earnest nonchalance that only an accomplished actor could pull off, "Do you think Jack would mind if we had an affair?"

I felt as if someone had just pushed the freeze-frame button on my life. I couldn't think and I couldn't answer. What I had dreamed of both asleep and awake was mere inches away, and I was entrapped by my silent confusion. Like me, I knew that he was in the last throes of a fading marriage and was as lonely as I was. I also knew the power of "sending"! How could I have been so stupid? Of course, he "picked up my thoughts." I was paralyzed with shock.

Whether it was morality that gripped my tongue or the dwindling hope that I could still keep my family intact only by staying within society's virtuous borders, I don't know. I remained as still as a doorstop, and Michael may have taken my complete lack of verbal skills as a polite, wordless turndown. We went to the theater in silence. It was a comedy. I know because everyone else in the theater was laughing. I saw nothing to laugh about.

Thinking back on that moment, and God knows I have, I don't know what would have happened had he just not mentioned Jack by name. It was only common sense that you don't kick-start an affair by throwing a husband's name into the mix. I returned alone to Los Angeles and tried to continue my day-to-day life as if nothing had happened, which, of course, was factual. But facts and the truth don't always line up, and the truth was that I could not erase that moment from my mind. Back and forth my thoughts went, weighing the pros and cons of an illicit romance. Since the cons were so obvious, I pushed them to one side and concentrated on the pros. I was crazy about him, yet he had used the word "affair," which goes well beyond the limits of "one-night stand" and implies a long and romantic future.

But not everything can be doled out for consideration. All I knew was that I was cold and alone and desperately needed someone to love me. I called Michael on a pay phone so that it would be impossible for our clandestine utterances ever to be traced. (I was already beginning to think like "the other woman.") He answered the phone and I floundered while trying to say the words I had been thinking about for weeks—those words that would make my thoughts real and my desires obvious.

"Were you serious when you asked if I wanted to have an affair?" I finally sputtered out. I don't know what I expected, but it certainly wasn't what I got.

He answered in the light, comedic tone that had made him a favorite to millions on the big screen. "I was just kidding around," Michael replied.

Whether his invitation in the hotel room was just a joke that I wasn't capable of getting at the time or his ego wasn't steeled for possible rejection, I'll never know. All I know is that that was the end of that. Having come so close myself, I didn't feel as if I had the right to blame Jack for any possible indiscretion on his part.

What my nonaffair with Michael did do was prove to me, once and for all, that my marriage was truly over. I hadn't been simply looking for momentary satisfaction in another man's arms. I wanted someone to love me, and now it was all too clear that my husband's heart had moved on permanently. And the crescendo of emotions I'd once felt for him were now just a faint and distant echo. I knew then that my marriage was over.

I finally understood the pain my mother had suffered through all those years. My husband had betrayed me in the same manner that my father had betrayed her. Mutual heartache can be a bridge between two people, but it definitely wasn't what I wanted to have in common with my mother.

I also knew that I was my father's daughter. What his reasons were for entering into all those extramarital relationships, I can't say. I don't know whether his excuses were similar to the ones I used, but I no longer felt in any position to judge his actions. And when I stopped viewing my father from my vantage point atop my high horse, I became free to simply love him for who he was, warts and all. With some embarrassment I had to accept the fact that warts ran in my family.

Jack and I tiptoed around our dead marriage the way

detectives do around a corpse. But eventually the inevitable must be addressed and dealt with. It was Jack who finally checked for a pulse and admitted out loud that our relationship no longer had a heartbeat. Never a master of good timing, Jack asked me for a separation on June 30, which happened to be our son's fourth birthday. (They always seem to "ask" for a separation, although questions don't get more rhetorical.) Although a separation implies that you both limp off into your own corner and take a needed breather, Jack and I were too intertwined in business to pull the threads apart that quickly.

On July 3 there was a premiere of *Who Framed Roger Rabbit*, which turned out to be a real family affair. I had been the one who found and negotiated the project for Jack's client, director Bob Zemeckis. Screams of laughter filled the packed theater, but I don't remember hearing them. With my daughter, Jesse, snuggled on my lap, my mind and heart couldn't have been further away from the joyful antics being played out onscreen.

Instead of joining in the revelry that surrounded me, I closed my eyes and silently prayed to God, *Please give me the strength to find another husband.* Then, as clear as if my eyes were wide open, I saw him in that moment. It was a vision of a man with white hair and wire-rimmed glasses, and he was smiling at me. It was the kind of warm, loving smile that somehow let me know that everything would be all right. I had never had a "vision" before that moment, and, as incongruous as it may have been, with Roger Rabbit raising comedic hell onscreen, I began to understand my connection to God in a new way. We really are protected.

It would prove vital as I found myself starting down the path to a new life.

Chapter Twelve

The Dark at the End of the Tunnel

Nobody ever chooses the already unfortunate as objects of his loyal friendship.

LUCAN

SEPARATIONS ARE NEVER EASY, but some are more difficult than others. Jack and I managed to do it the worst way possible: We separated while remaining to live together. This idea was neither his nor mine; it was my therapist's, who could say it with such psychological authority only because she didn't have to live with us. She told us not to move from the house until Jack found a new home. We had agreed to co-custody (a decision that filled me with intense grief and guilt, even though I knew it was right). We were told by my analyst that "Children that young need to *see* where they were going to live." Perhaps, but it was what we were all feeling for the next two months before Jack actually packed his bags and left that hurt me the most.

Jack and I did our best to appear the same as usual, but nothing was the same anymore and the usual was anything but. In our quest for outward normalcy, we even shared the same bed, where old acquaintances had definitely been forgotten, and it would have been comedic if either of us could remember how to laugh.

Children have an uncanny antenna for picking up moods and emotions. As adults we can try to act like nothing has changed, pouring them orange juice and flipping their pancakes, but they know better. They're like little thermometers that can always tell when the weather has changed. Jessica was six years old and Aaron was four, and they could see through our Norman Rockwell act with heartbreaking clarity. Even our pet, Misty, a Seeing Eye dog that had been drummed out of service due to her penchant for chasing cars, gave way to melancholia.

Jessica's reaction to the silent turmoil was to take control of her tiny world. She would insist on getting dressed without any help from me, throwing together fabrics and colors that would embarrass a scarecrow. I allowed her to do this, realizing her need to express her emotions in one of the few ways available to her. For some miraculous reason, these discordant outfits always seemed to work the moment she had them on.

Aaron didn't feel the same need to map out his own world

but quietly wondered where he fit in to the one that was breaking apart. One night when I was tucking him into bed, Aaron looked up and from those little-boy quivering lips asked, "Who do you love more, me or God?"

I prayed long and hard on that one. Maybe too long and too hard. I finally came up with an answer that I felt would satisfy him, not wanting him left feeling the need to go toe-to-toe with God over my affection. "Loving you is loving God," I replied in that soothing manner that mothers use to placate children and end conversations. I could tell from his facial response that this was the answer he neither expected nor wanted. I assumed he had asked because he witnessed me praying much more than he ever had before, lighting candles at an altar I had erected. Often Aaron would sit beside me, closing his eyes and squeezing his little body in an attempt to invoke the spirit. Perhaps the answer I gave him was the thoughtful, correct one. Still, you can't expect a four-year-old to get metaphysical, and now I wish I had simply hugged him and said, "I love you more," which is all he wanted to hear.

What I had failed to recognize was that his father and I, though neither of us consciously realized it, were both sending him the same message in our tone and in our actions: "please love me more," turning the breakdown of his world into a contest, with him as the prize. The last thing he needed was to feel that he was also in competition with God.

Aaron pronounced Irma, our nanny's name, like "Eeema" ("Mother" in Hebrew—believe me, it was not lost on me). He did not display sadness. His kindergarten teacher thought he might have ADD; we had him tested. His jumping around was half "boy" and maybe half trying to be a superhero. He would don his cape and stand at the top of the stairwell four steps above Misty, our golden retriever. Misty was elderly, sweet, and depressed, like everyone else in the house. Most of the time she just lay about, but during this time, her special spot put her in mortal danger. As she lay tucked into where the floor and first step met, Aaron would fly in his "feetie" Dr. Denton PJs and cape above the four steps hoping to fly past Misty's body.

Misty had been a cuddlemate for Aaron since he was a rug rat. Aaron would splay her open to her back, nestle his head on her tummy, suck his thumb, twirl her hair, and fall asleep. His strawberry blond curls exactly matched the color and soft-ness of her mane; some well-meaning idiot teased him that Misty was his mommy. This time Misty was in danger from her biggest love. Aaron was attempting to fly so as to clear four large steps and one large dog's body safely to the rug below. Misty leaped, threatening to bite Aaron, and the long-lived love affair ended. No longer was dog man's best friend.

The innocence of their love ended. Misty became Kryp-tonite. What was once his home now could kill him. He was decisive, and even now at four he made up his mind. It did not matter that he was the instigator/perpetrator; he would not risk the bite. Might was enough, as far as being hurt. I guess Aaron had witnessed that "might" could lead to eventuality.

Being a superhero, there was a chance to save all of our days.

I asked Aaron what he wanted to be when he grew up. He thought about it for quite some time, looked up, and said, "I want to save people. I quickly said, "Well, you can save people by being a fireman, a policeman, a forest ranger, a lifeguard. . . . How do you want to save people?" Aaron quickly said, "I want to be a rope."

One morning after putting on my makeup, along with my best "everything is just fine" look, Jess woke up and shared her dream with me. I watched her little face as she described a frog and a turtle having a big fight over a lily pad. "Then God came down and cut the lily pad in two, so they could each have a piece to live on," she said. I realized then that my six-year-old knew more about how to deal with separation than my therapist.

When Jack and I finally cut the tattered cord and divorced, the inevitable happened; almost all our mutual show-business friends immediately hopped onto my ex-husband's side of the fence. (No one even bothered with the pretense of straddling.) Naturally, this kind of friendship hopping isn't unusual anywhere, but in Hollywood the smell of success is the most powerful of perfumes, and as one of the top agents in town, Jack had all the power.

Did I hate any of them because overnight my name was erased from their address books?

Certainly I was hurt, but I can't say that I was surprised. I understood their desertion and why my phone calls weren't being returned by those I had once thought of as intimates. As far as human traits go, loyalty doesn't rank high on the industry's list of importance. "My friends" quite simply no longer considered me a part of getting them a deal.

My sense of desolation wasn't helped as I prepared to spend my first Christmas alone as a divorced woman. Jack, overcome with a weekend father's desire to play Santa Claus to the kids, had taken the children and flown to Hawaii for the holidays. Christmas affects us all, whatever our religion and our beliefs happen to be. At its heart, Christmas is an emotion, and one that, more often than not, is tinged with melancholia.

Not wishing to spend the holidays staring at a silent telephone or busying myself dancing around the sinkhole of depression I could feel myself sliding into, I hopped a plane for Bora Bora, which like New York City, is so nice they named it twice. The entire island appeared like something from Gauguin's brush: lush tropical foliage, turquoise water, and volcanic mountains in the distance, too easygoing to bother belching up lava. I gratefully assumed there would be no mistletoe hanging, under which I could feel the absence of no one wanting to kiss me.

The bounce in geography did nothing to lighten my mood, and I spent my days in paradise alternating between crying and healing. (Although I have since come to learn that they are, in fact, part of the same fabric, and you can't have one without the other.) For me, music is a magic carpet for the psyche, and so instead of listening to Christmas carols, I inundated myself in Basia's "Time and Tide," "A New Day for You," and "Brave New Hope." They lifted my spirits sufficiently so that I could at least do a little sightseeing.

One afternoon, taking a trip by catamaran, the tour sailor, noting I was alone, took pity on me. He invited me to visit his commune situated on a tiny private island. With nothing else to do on Christmas, I accepted. The commune itself was a series of tents held together by patches and the grace of God. Its members numbered fifty, coming from all over the world. Their hair was long and their clothes tie-dyed, giving them the appearance of hippies who couldn't scrape together enough money to get into a Grateful Dead concert. The majority of them were in their midthirties, having glued themselves together in location and belief since they were eighteen. Most of them came from troubled families, left home early, and instead of college chose to expand their mental horizons by following their leader, IO, pronounced "Yo." He was in his fifties and presented himself as a communicator/descendant of extraterrestrial wisdom.

These unorthodox convictions suited those who followed him, and in short order the tribe became convinced that they, too, had arrived here on Earth from another solar system. The spot not on any map that they zeroed in on as their place of origin was Pleiades, and they had arrived here with the ability to transmute energy. Considering the earthly homes they had all escaped from, any other part of the galaxy must have seemed preferable. Ridiculous? Perhaps. And maybe I should have beat it out of there before I was fitted for a coconut-shell beanie with antennae. But it's not in my nature to pull down the curtain of judgment before I've listened. Truly listened.

All my life I've been an open ear for the beliefs of others. That certainly doesn't mean I will blindly accept those beliefs as my own, but there's a thirst in me that demands I take it all in with a respectful, curious, and open mind. And, I must admit, at that point in my life I was interested in any other world that wasn't my own for Christmas. As I got to know these people, whether their roots of origin were in Pleiades or Pittsburgh, I found them to be warm, intelligent, and deeply dedicated to their beliefs. It wasn't one of those fly-by-night communes made popular in the sixties where hippies drifted through for a few weeks to grow some corn and get laid. They had been a tightly woven surrogate family for eighteen years, and I was more than a little touched and honored for them to so graciously take me in and accept me as one of their own.

After living so many years in Los Angeles, where cults popped up with the regularity of bubbles in boiling water, I would be lying to say that I didn't have some trepidation when accepting their invitation. But my fears were quickly extinguished. There was no brainwashing involved, but a freewheeling exchange of ideas shared on one of the most idyllic spots on earth. Whether one agreed or not, it was that individual's choice, and there was no attempt to bend any of my precepts in any direction they didn't want to go. I was free to listen, and listen I did.

The more I listened, the more I realized that, no matter what planet you're from or believe you're from, every life-form in the galaxy is after the same thing: really good sex.

For the men, holding back their sperm became of vital importance. The goal was to reverse their orgasm through an understanding of tantric teachings, controlling the energetic combustion of their climax—in short, keeping the firecracker lit without it going off. From what I hear, that is no easy feat. Women were also taught to harness their orgasmic convulsing and release their seismic energy through the crown of their heads. I don't care what part of the galaxy you're from, a woman's orgasm is hard to come by, and I could see there was no way the majority of women were going to change course when we felt one coming down the pike.

Camelot's Round Table was created circular to illustrate that everyone who sat there was equal—a really swell idea, but all the knights knew that wherever King Arthur sat was really the head of the table. After all, they were wearing helmets, not blinders. And in this commune of equals, IO was the leader, and pleasing him and meeting his standards allowed one the great honor of sitting closer to him. If you really hit the jackpot, you were given the privilege of making love to him. Having multiple partners was another one of the perks he bestowed upon himself. He must have reasoned, what was the point of coming all the way from another planet if you have to be faithful?

Although the freshly wounded feminist in me got her hackles up watching behavior not dissimilar to what I saw in Hollywood, I was nevertheless intrigued. I listened in earnest to discover if any of their ideas could lead me down paths I felt I needed to travel. I was from Florida, not Pleiades; a nice Jewish girl who believed in faithfulness, even though I hadn't been the beneficiary of great role models.

They were vegetarians, while there was nothing I enjoyed more than diving headfirst into a thick steak on the bone. It had been a great Christmas and would make a wonderful story to tell when I got back to Los Angeles, but I didn't yet realize that these warm, loving, albeit socially dissonant people would change my life.

I had irrationally jumped on a plane to Tahiti in a mad rush to get away from it all. It never dawned on me that I would be returning to L.A. a few weeks later with a new set of building blocks with which to begin both seeing life and living it. It was just one more lesson in how Divine design knows exactly what it's doing.

I was at my most vulnerable, with all confidence in myself having seemingly evaporated. Over the following days, some of the most personally intense I've ever spent, my dietary habits changed, and I went from loving short ribs to becoming a vegetarian. Although this alteration in my culinary life made me feel stronger and more energized, it was nothing that numerous Beverly Hills wives hadn't attempted, but they still remained miserable.

What that strange, caring group of people gathered away in a little commune on Bora Bora taught me was how to find the courage to journey inside the deepest, darkest parts of myself and, for the first time, truly meditate. By its very nature meditation is a form of self-love, because we're actually taking the time to connect with our deepest thoughts and emotions.

Most people think about themselves all the time. It's only natural. But truly getting in touch with yourself is an entirely different matter. When you open yourself, you are, in fact, opening yourself up to the universe. After all, we are all connected. Elevate your own consciousness and elevate all the worlds.

In those few mystical days on that island paradise, they had expanded my belief system to see that what I had never been taught might, indeed, be possible. I was searching. Constantly searching. There were more horizons out there than I had ever imagined. And breaking down some old rigidity never hurt anybody.

On my return it was time for me to take stock of whatever stock I had left. I had loved being a wife and a loyal friend, and taken nourishment from both. Now that both those watering holes had suddenly dried up, I concentrated completely on the blessings I still did have: my children and my beliefs of guidance, protection, and God.

I love my two children equally (I know, I know—every mother says that) and appreciate them in different ways for their various attributes and character traits. My son, Aaron, the youngest, went to NYU film school and has always had a filmmaker streak running through his boyish nature, much like his father. But, unlike Jack, he's never had to live in fear of not making a living, nor felt the economic need to cut his dreams off at the knees in pursuit of the dollar.

Now that he's grown, my son is a film writer/director, talking about it with the same enthusiasm as his father did when he took me out on our first date and we dined happily on two appetizers. I think of Aaron as a realistic dreamer, with an originality and brilliance of his own. He has a rapier wit and a true film lover's photographic memory for dialogue, credits, and shots. Best of all, his heart is kind, and for that I'm grateful.

My daughter, Jessica, is also wickedly artistic. I believe she is a genius—a visio-spatial genius. Her understanding of three-dimensional design—furniture, art, architecture, and textiles—defies normal convention of interior decor. Jessica also graduated from NYU film school, but in dedication to her husband and son, she is a full-time mom and a part-time interior decorator. Jessica has always had more of my spiritual bent to her nature, giving us an invisible connection that binds us without words. Jesse was only a year and a half old when my grandmother, Lucy, held her in her arms for the last time. Yet, when my daughter was old enough to speak, she would always talk about Lucy. There was no apparent reason that Lucy held such prominence for my daughter, except that Lucy was Jessica's guide.

Jesse and I went to art camp when she was seven years old. The teacher gave an assignment to paint a portrait from our mind's eye. We were told just to use "flow" to render a human face. I have always loved art, although the feelings have never been mutual. Without my knowledge of what was about to appear on the canvas, I painted Lucy. The profile that my hand had created was of this young woman's face and hairdo. She was the spitting image of an old photograph of my youthful grandmother. I did not know her then. I was stunned that my unconscious would bring her at this youthful age to my fingertips.

But the aftershock had an even greater impact on me, when Jesse immediately asked for the painting to hang in her room. It was then that I came to realize that our guides like us to know who they are. When she was alive, my French grandmother had always been enormously vain; I can only assume she had refused to visit this plane unless she looked a hell of a lot better than when she left it. Our guides want the contact. It's up to us to simply invite them in.

As a divorced mother I felt the weight of nurturing both my children and my professional livelihood, and it was then that the Fates seemed to cut me a break. Fairly quickly, while under contract to Warner Bros. for three and a half years and then 20th Century Fox for three and a half years, I produced *Lucky Stiff*, *Vital Signs*, and *Big Girls Don't Cry*. None of these films were box office enough for a studio to renew or house my production company. I was forced to be truly independent.

I caught another wave of good luck. Immediately I set up projects all over town with major muscled talent, including Tom Cruise, Ron Howard, Bob Zemeckis, and Sidney Pollack.

It sounds impressive, and, indeed, it was. The trouble is in the phrase "set up projects." That only means that those glittering names are interested, but the studio has not yet committed to a green light. It's the greased loophole that many Hollywood dreams have slid through and vanished.

Then the Fates decided to drop me like a hot potato.

For a maze of various reasons, each and every one of these

projects that I had infused with all of my hopes and energy fizzled. (Many years later, I was an uncredited producer of *Man from Elysian Fields*.) I am convinced that all the successful people in show business, whether they're actors, writers, directors, or producers, are basically children at heart. By that I mean their hearts beat with a child's blind optimism, without being hampered by either an adult's common sense or rational thought giving lie to their fantasies. We sustain on the vapors of dreams. In my time in the business I have taken more than my share of body blows, and it was my child's enthusiasm for making movies that kept me buoyant. The slings and arrows of reality were no more than an obstacle course to maneuver around until I reached my ultimate goal.

My optimism, along with my career, began to sink. My speedy descent was accelerated when my most beloved of projects, *Trollops*, lost its director, Sidney Pollack, and was suddenly homeless. Every one of my projects was meaningful to me, but *Trollops* was a passion that had mushroomed into a feverish obsession. Told in the style of Restoration comedy, the nuts and bolts of the story were true, dealing with that moment in the seventeenth century when women were finally permitted to act on the English stage. (For years women were banned from appearing on the boards, and all female roles were portrayed by boys, which must have driven casting directors crazy.) Because there were no established actresses around at that time, prostitutes were often hired as female thespians.

In 1985, *Trollops* was the very first project I fell in love with as a new producer. Now, seven years later, I was still determined. I went from studio to studio trying to find a new home for my baby, and though everyone was fascinated by the tale, no one was interested in producing it. Then along came *Shakespeare in Love*. Why, when we were first, did this script suddenly get the green light?

During the following months, I seesawed between two emotions. Some days I was angry; other days I was depressed. But I was never deterred, and my willingness to grovel to get this movie made finally paid off. Propaganda Films took pity on me, opening up its coffers to the tune of five thousand dollars and allowing me to direct and shoot a five-minute director's test scene of *Trollops* for them. True, it wasn't the kind of heavyweight deal I had been accustomed to making in my days as an agent, but that didn't matter. Only one thing mattered to me now: I was finally going to get another chance to be a director.

The first thing I did was call in every show-business chit I had collected over my career, and the happy result was that I had some of the best in the business agreeing to work for this neophyte director gratis. Those five minutes of celluloid became the focal point of my life, and I was as careful and precise as a diamond cutter chiseling away at a priceless bauble. I storyboarded every frame, cast it with Adrienne Shelly, and assembled an all-star crew of professional friends to back me up behind the camera.

I prepared and prepared, and when I had done all that I could conceivably do, I prepared some more. Then I did one more thing not usually found in the director's handbook: Before a frame of film was shot, I called on the spirit of Bob Fosse and asked for guidance. In my opinion, he was one of the supreme film directors (*Cabaret* and *All That Jazz* are only two of the jewels in his cinematic legacy), and his was the soul I wanted to tap into before embarking on what I now thought of as the fulfillment of my life's quest. I set up my altar, lit the candles, and went deep into meditation, asking him for answers.

Directing those five minutes turned out to be some of the hardest work I've ever done, as well as the most gratifying. I don't remember sleeping. Why would I want to, when being awake was so joyous? I was giving life to my dream. Perhaps producing was so hard because I was meant to direct.

If this was one of those Hollywood stories we all grew up watching, the kind my mother took me to see when I was a little girl living in Florida, this tale would most assuredly have a happy ending. All those utopian notions I had in film school to someday be the voice behind the camera would have resulted in lavish critical acclaim and a cascading windfall of green at the box office. But, as it happened, those five minutes of film I'd given birth to, loved, and nurtured turned out to be slow, dull, banal, and lifeless.

It always hurts whenever a dream that you've clung to for years finally dies with a resounding thud, but it is particularly painful when you can sit there and watch that failure over and over again, like turning a corkscrew slowly into your own heart. Although I've relived it thousands of times, I'm still not quite sure exactly what went wrong. (As comforting as it may be, there is no one to blame but myself for its shimmering mediocrity.) Being completely honest, I must accept the fact that it's more than possible that I simply lacked the talent that I'd always imagined was sitting dormant inside me just waiting for the opportunity to spring to life.

You may be asking the same question I asked myself: Where the hell was Bob Fosse when I needed him? Doesn't this lack of inspiration in itself turn the whole idea of help from the other side on its head?

Channeling or mediumship can't perform miracles. As Roy Scheider, Fosse's alter ego in *All That Jazz* tells an aspiring dancer, "I can't make you a great dancer. I don't even know if I can make you a good dancer. But if you let me, I can make you a better dancer." There is no guarantee that your prayers will be answered. Years later, Bob did come to me. On the other side, at the same time I was directing my test, he had been working on himself. The souls on the request end usually want to help; they want to be of service, but it may not be theirs to do. They often go to "school" after they pass, to find self-love and the meaning of their lives. In short, not every dead person is available to satisfy your needs. My guidance realm would have steered me elsewhere if I had truly been meant to make better directing choices.

For example, my director of photography was John Lindley. *Field of Dreams* was one of his finest works. He advised me to troll the studio's prop shops for visual enrichment for a scene we would shoot in a meadow. My meditation told me that props weren't necessary. As I watched my short film later, that scene turned out to be part of the obvious bland result. Would a haystack and baskets have saved the film? Of course not, but I did realize I had chosen not to listen to my talented advisor here on earth; I was more interested in proving that I had an angel on my shoulder.

My incompetence as a director didn't deter me from trust in the other side. Obviously, my greater goal was not directing, but to expand my knowledge of the guidance realm. What it can do is open you up, allowing the other world to spark the needs and possibilities within yourself. As the saying goes, God writes straight with crooked lines. When all doors close, there is another plan; God just hadn't revealed it to me yet.

✦   ✦   ✦

Early mornings in Los Angeles I like to take a walk along the beach with my dog, Ferris. He's part terrier and part anything else his ancestors could mix and match. I've watched him scamper along the ocean and I've found myself envying him. Ferris, like all animals, lives in the moment. Dogs concentrate on the tree they're smelling or the food they're eating, giving absolutely no concern to the woes of yesterday or the pitfalls of tomorrow. Human beings go through their days doing the exact opposite.

When examining our lives, we often try to see past the

immediate and concentrate on our outstretched dreams for our future. It can come in very handy, giving us a finish line to strain for even when the winds are blowing against us. And when our everyday reality changes, we are usually flexible enough to change with it, as long as the goal we're after remains intact, if only in our imagination.

In short order, both my marriage and my career had crumbled under my feet. As difficult as it was, I could accept it. I could chalk it up as the downside of being alive and somehow muster the strength to go on. But when the dream you have been clinging to for years suddenly shatters, going on can feel like a pointless and lonely exercise. Still, I was a working woman with two young children, and so I continued working in the only business I knew.

Chapter Thirteen

My Last Stand

What is there more of in the world
than anything else? Ends.

CARL SANDBURG

IT'S SO DAMNED EASY TO GET DEPRESSED. We concentrate on our failures, our near misses, and the what-ifs, which never seem to be in short supply. Fortunately, once I finished with my self-flagellation, I concentrated on my two children.

Whatever had gone wrong in my life, whatever bad decisions I'd made, I had done something wonderfully right. No matter what lay ahead, I knew I'd already gotten more out of life than I could ever have dreamed of when I was a little girl living her world inside the four walls of her tiny bedroom. After that personal and professional debacle, I filled my time by floundering, a desperate act that gives a drowning man the illusion that he'll make it to shore.

I still had my bagful of embryonic ideas that I was busily trying to midwife to life. One planned screenplay that didn't make it to film, though I consider the experience a success for personal reasons, was *The Angel of Death*, about a nurse in a hospital who helped people die. It was penned by Alan Brennert, who was one of the writers of the television revival of *Twilight Zone*.

No one can take part in Rod Serling's legacy without being attuned to worlds outside our own. Besides being both gifted and intelligent, Alan was open to the unexplainable, and we forged a special bond between us. As the title of our proposed film suggests, he, too, was well acquainted with death and believed in the bridge that connects our realm with the next. He'd had a girlfriend who had been very sick, and as they traveled together through her lingering illness toward her eventual death, she told him who she wanted at her funeral.

After she died, Alan did as she wished, but there was one young man she had very much wanted to attend the funeral for whom Alan simply couldn't find any contact information, no matter how hard he searched. He fingered her Rolodex cards dozens of times with no luck. The next morning, waking from a fitful sleep, the first thing he did was to glance over at the Rolodex.

Alan still found it amazing to remember as he told me the story, but the one and only card exposed was that with the name of the friend she had so desperately wanted at her funeral.

Alan was convinced that the other side not only communicates with us, but assists us in a physical way. In a business built on make-believe, it was stirring to work with someone who believed as deeply as I did.

Still, it was no secret around town that I hadn't produced a film in seven years, and I was now looked on by many executives as a pesky fly that still managed to buzz and bother them. If I were to survive in this business, I knew I'd have to rely on the skills I had honed as an agent at CAA, finding young, promising talent whose careers, I could feel, were ready to explode.

One of those hungry talents was Toby Emmerich, a young executive at New Line who was a damn good writer. Toby was fresh and green and eager, and I took an immediate liking to him. He had written a script entitled *Frequency* that I was anxious to produce and guided through numerous rewrites. We spent countless hours brainstorming and arguing and laughing. With each alteration the script got better. I found just watching Toby's enthusiasm was contagious. I gave the script to Greg Hoblit to direct. I could feel some of the old excitement come over me once again.

My life changed suddenly and forever at my son's bar mitzvah, that great day when every Jewish mother celebrates her son becoming a man and secretly wishes he'd remain a little boy. The guest list was long. Since the divorce, many of our old friends were strangers to me, but without rancor or recrimination, I greeted them all with open arms. I was not about to let anything spoil this night.

Howard Koch Jr., son of an ex-Paramount chief, was there because he was my personal friend, and we had development projects together. Greg Hoblit had been invited because he was my friend. We, too, had development projects together. Greg had other plans that night. Having gone over the seating chart innumerable times, I decided to seat Howard next to Toby, knowing that a young exec would be thrilled listening to the tales of old Tinseltown that Howard was so good at spinning.

It was a glorious night as the champagne and the laughter and the tears of joy all flowed in equal measure. And as I danced across the floor plumped with pride, I was blissfully unaware of the Machiavellian screwing I was in the process of getting. My great friend Howard Koch Jr. was in a heated discussion with Toby Emmerich, laying the groundwork for how it would be in the best interests of both of them to let him produce Toby's script and cut me out of the cinematic equation completely. Howard explained that he knew Greg "better."

Toby was more than willing to agree to this literary mutiny before the waiters came around with dessert.

Granted, loyalty has always been a transient bond at best in Hollywood. Still, I don't think I'm setting my standards too high when I say backstabbing reaches a new low when you do it to your dear friend at her own son's bar mitzvah. (I spoke to Howard one last time after that, demanding an explanation. His simple reply, said without even the slightest twinge of guilt, was "I have always been in the shadow of my father and I need all the credit I can get.")

Was I bitter? Bitterness was practically leaking out of my pores. Had I gone in for an X-ray I'm quite sure the doctor would see my organs tying themselves into knots. After seven long and lonely years trying to piece a movie together, my good and trusted friend had blithely sold me out because he had unresolved issues with his father. The never-ending acid thoughts I had of Mr. Koch Jr. and Mr. Emmerich were burning a rut through my brain.

The old bromide that "revenge is sweet" may be true. I don't know. What I do know is that constantly thinking about it can wear a hole through your soul. My revenge fantasies began to fade when it dawned on me how many hours and days and weeks I had spent thinking about them while I was certain they hadn't spent even a single moment of their time thinking about me. All I was managing to accomplish was to waste more of my life obsessing over people I never wanted to see or speak to again.

When I finally realized this, the flow of bile that had been gurgling through me stopped immediately. Bitterness is one of the most depleting of all human emotions, and we always seem to spend it on those least deserving of our feelings of any kind. *Frequency* was eventually made, without my participation. This act of betrayal by two of my most trusted friends was the final straw in what had become an enormous and daunting haystack. Besides the lies, the forgotten promises, and the broken hopes, the work had simply become too hard for no result. The day my son became a man was the same day I left the business.

Chapter Fourteen

I Guess I'll Have to Change My Plans

When you feel your song is orchestrated wrong,
why should you prolong your stay?

NOËL COWARD

THE MOST IMPORTANT WORD IN THE ABOVE TITLE is "change," which very well may be the most frightening group of letters in the English language. Naturally, we all want particular elements of our life to change. We just don't want to dig our way through that dark, long, and lonely tunnel to change them. We'd much prefer change to suddenly show up at our front door, like a package from UPS.

Whether I wanted to or not, at this time in my life I knew I had to shift direction and alter my chosen path. I had to ask myself why I was working in a business where even my most trusted friends were not above a little treachery if it was to their benefit. And why was I picking them to be my most trusted friends? This was a family pattern that again and again needed breaking.

As long as I could remember, I had been pulled in two distinctly diverse directions by my passions of psychiatry and art. The one that I chose had been a mental flip of the coin, and art had won. What would have happened, all those years ago, had my father said no when I begged him to let me go to film school? Had I allowed my own ego and rose-colored visions of glory to take me down the wrong path? Film school, becoming an agent, and working as a producer were all steps to get me to a place I now realized I could never reach. And, more important, no longer cared to reach.

Each of our lives is a glaringly white canvas waiting to be filled, and we do it dot by intricate dot, much like a Georges Seurat painting. And, like a work by that artist, it's vital that we are able to step back and take it all in before we can clearly see what it is we've created. Only then can we fully understand what the canvas of our life truly needs.

Now, as a middle-aged divorced woman with a career that had everything but a chalk outline around it, I had to stand back and honestly examine what I had created for my life—and what I wanted that next dot to be. To reassess the pivotal choices we have made in life is a grueling, arduous process, almost guaranteed to leave us feeling emotionally drained and scared and overly wary of our next step. If we have made so many wrong decisions in the past, we ask ourselves, how can we possibly know that the next one will be right?

First, you scour yourself for lessons needed, and if in your heart you cannot find a lesson in the bad choices or choices not garnered, perhaps God has another plan. But we do know that remaining stuck in a bad life like an insect on flypaper can never be right. Never. We usually have to so hate where we are that we are willing to risk the fear of change. So often we stay with things long after we know they're wrong only because of the amount of time and hardship we have already poured into them. Marriages, jobs, and friendships can all be chaff that we allow ourselves to confuse with wheat simply because we're afraid of letting them go.

We have to ask ourselves what type of future we desire, that personal goal we want to reach that too often has been allowed to sit dormant inside of us and slowly atrophy. Once we can untangle those emotions and lay out our true aspirations and hibernating ambitions in front of us like a map, then whatever choices we make to get to our goal will be the right choices.

By its very nature, change is growth. Granted, change is hardly ever easy; a caterpillar must go through his share of Sturm und Drang before finally making it out of the cocoon as a butterfly. But can anyone who has ever watched a butterfly flit its multicolored wings against a blue summer sky doubt that the metamorphosis it went through was worth it?

Whenever we hit the brick wall where our choices have led us, the first thing we usually do is kick ourselves for having been so stupid. This emotional and mental punishment doesn't change anything but adds another thick coating of depression to a psyche already swaybacked with guilt. Did I tumble into this pit? Of course. There's really no way to avoid it. The trick then becomes how long it takes us to climb out.

There's a moment in everyone's life when we become all too aware of time passing. Perhaps it's the mirrored reflection of those crow's-feet crinkled around the eyes that weren't there yesterday or that instant we notice we're no longer climbing the stairs two steps at a time. Whatever the case, time becomes a tangible element in our lives, and we are suddenly very aware of wasting it.

And self-pity, hands down the most self-indulgent of emotions, is nothing other than a waste of our valuable time. That having been said, I plead guilty for having done my share of wallowing. Self-pity has a way of sneaking up on us, like a hungry cat. Our mistake is that we feed it. We then slide into the grieving process, painfully plucking the same emotional strings we do as when someone we love has passed on. This is only natural, as it's impossible to escape the feeling that we are allowing a part of ourselves to die. But, as any gardener knows, there are times when certain branches of a plant must be severed if that plant is to eventually flourish.

F. Scott Fitzgerald said, "There are no second acts in American life." That sounds thoughtful and deep and tragically poetic. The only problem with it is that it just isn't true. Each of us can decide whether our bad choices in life (and we've all made them) will be chains that bind us to our past or if they'll be used as the necessary building blocks to change our lives and understand the strengths that were born out of the lessons.

When we can begin to accomplish this in our own minds, a seismic miracle starts to take place. We find we can no longer regret our mistakes, as it's the knowledge they have given us that allows us to finally flex new muscles, break down rigidity, or reshape a worldview. It felt like a lifetime ago that I had attended film school as an eager young woman, naively chomping at the bit to bend the boundaries of cinema. Now, as a divorced, unemployed mother of two, I decided to continue my education. But this time I would go to school to get my doctorate of clinical psychology. After all, my mother's death inspired me to bring a new idea of life after life and intuition to psychology. What was I waiting for?

Although we may not recognize it when it's taking place, there seems to be a perfect symmetry to life, and though I often felt at loose ends as I attempted to lay out a new path toward an unimagined future, I began to recognize that I had, in fact, really come full circle.

Chapter Fifteen

Field Trips

*The fairest thing we can experience
is the mysterious. It is the fundamental emotion
which stands at the cradle of true art and true science.*

ALBERT EINSTEIN

WITH MY OWN NEWLY PRINTED DIVORCE DECREE signaling the end to an enormous chapter of my life, I had to hop a plane and fly to Manhattan to attend the wedding of my last remaining mutual friends and Jack's client Robert Kamen. Although I would have much preferred to curl up on my couch, a blanket over my legs with a spoon in one hand and a gallon of Häagen Dazs's Belgian Chocolate Chocolate ice cream in the other, I had promised to be there, and made a vow to myself that I would act appropriately gleeful. A recent divorcee is never a welcome addition to a wedding ceremony, and you almost feel as if you have to explain to the newlyweds that divorce is not a communicable disease.

When I arrived in New York I went to my hotel room and collapsed into bed. Between the jet lag and my own fragile state, it wasn't difficult falling asleep. It was waking up that proved to be the problem. When I finally did arise, it was noon, and I had slept for an astounding twelve hours.

In the old days before voice mail and blinking lights, a hotel would use pink slips to deliver messages. There were three or four pink slips waiting for me under the door (which means the phone would have rung approximately four times for each pink slip). Although I had been tired, it was hard for me to believe I had slept through all those rings. Raising two children, I had become accustomed to waking up at the slightest noise.

I got out of bed and hurried to the bathroom to wash my face. There does come a time in every woman's life when she doesn't want to look at her reflection first thing in the morning, particularly before her initial cup of coffee or dabbing on some makeup. In my panic I had obviously forgotten the rules, and when I glanced at myself in the mirror I saw a thin, small, short, red blood mark on my right lower lid, as though from a scalpel incision.

And then I remembered the dream that woke me from my marathon sleep. The figure of a man dressed neatly in a business suit was shaking my hand as if to greet me. He had a strong, commanding grip, and as I looked down at his hand, I saw that he only had three fingers. It was then that he told me he was from outer space, and as he continued to squeeze my hand I became a squidlike being swimming in some gelatinous substance. Then I felt this presence imploring me to not let "them" get near my eyes! "Don't let them get near your eyes," kept echoing around me until it jolted me awake. Whatever I had just experienced would have to wait. The unexplainable, after all, takes some time to sort out, and I had a wedding to get to. All I remember from the event was that a number of the other guests complimented me on my appearance, saying that I glowed. Either they were being polite or a paranormal experience is good for the complexion.

It was all too strange for me not to research the experience I felt I had been through. And, as is the case with most phenomena, the more I researched, the stranger it became. Like a reporter, the presumed glitter of being a film producer allowed me to examine all sorts of back alleys of interest, with people more than willing to volunteer their knowledge to my exploration.

After attending the wedding, I left New York and headed for Tucson. The journey wasn't because I had any great love of cactus, but it was within throwing distance of Roswell, the area where whispers had always insisted a spaceship had crashed in the 1950s, which supposedly led to the greatest cover-up in our government's history. I don't remember whether I said I was planning to make a film about that mysterious event or what, but I'm sure that's the impression I gave. It's a very handy impression to give when you want people to open up.

Through meeting various people, I became friendly with a retired army colonel. (I've found that those in the business of keeping secrets, after they've retired, can become downright chatterboxes. After all, even the face behind Watergate's Deep Throat eventually peeked out from behind his self-imposed curtain.) I trusted the colonel, and it wasn't long before he trusted me. There was someone, he said, he thought I should meet. He introduced me to a widow of a military man who had been murdered under mysterious circumstances. After a few quick pleasantries, she began to unleash her heart to me.

She insisted that her husband had been killed because he knew the facts surrounding the enigma that was Roswell, and he felt he couldn't keep silent any longer. There was nothing wide-eyed in her telling of her tale. In fact, she had a warm, gentle face that reminded me of television's Aunt Bee making her story sound all the more reasonable. Now, whether what she told me was true or not, I can't say with any definitive certainty. But I can say that she believed it, and this was a sensible, feet-on-the-ground woman whose imagination didn't operate outside the confines of her five senses.

As she talked I took into account that crazy people often have a way of acting sane, eventually making you wonder if you're not the one who's truly crazy. So, as she continued talking, I made it a point to keep glancing over at the colonel, whose level head matched his flattop. I searched for any slight sign on his face or tiny gesture that would indicate that he believed the loss of her husband may have pushed her mentally over the brink. I found none, and the more she talked, the more I was convinced that the colonel was convinced.

As in most things, I did my best to remain skeptical. It's that healthy dose of questioning that makes whatever answers you eventually reach at the end of your journey solid and real and custom-tailored to fit your own sensibilities. I still had more questions, and using my passport of being a producer, I began to speak to scientists about their beliefs concerning the experience I'd had in that Manhattan hotel room. I'd half expected them to laugh at me, pat my head condescendingly, and tell me to go back to Hollywood where such incredible flights of fancy were best served up with a bucket of popcorn and a gallon of soda.

What amazed me most was that the majority of them weren't amazed at all. I was startled to find that among these highly educated, grounded intellectuals there is a common consensus that we have been, and continue to be, visited not only by beings from other planets, but also consciousness from other dimensions. I was told that there have been countless incidences, all of them well documented and eerily similar to my own, in which people have awakened after long, deep sleeps of losing time with memories of abductions. The scientists I spoke to could only conclude that these "beings" attempt to connect with us.

Since then I've seen film of the autopsy performed on the aliens that had crashed in Roswell, with all of their internal organs exactly where ours are located. Every expert I know in the craft of celluloid insists that there are no special effects and the footage could not have been doctored. I came to believe, after listening to and digesting all the information I had been given, that, in my experience in that Manhattan hotel room when I was asleep and vulnerable, a "guiding" consciousness came to protect me, and is very much with me all the time.

You wouldn't think of going to bed at night without checking the windows and locking the front door, a way of guarding ourselves when we're asleep and at our most defenseless. Prayer can be the most impenetrable of protective shields, and we all have the ability to bring in, with demand, consciousness to safeguard us against unwanted interdimensional abduction or interference.

At one time or another we have all felt something "off" around us, as if we were shrouded in uncomfortable energy. To dispel this unwanted field we must openly, with demand (either out loud or in our heads) ask and invite the dark to be transmuted to light. If there are visiting outside "dark" forces, invite them to be of the light, or simply ask them to leave. Ask your battalion of angels to sweep the room. Tell the dissonant energies that they can use your experiences, your assistance on the dream plane, but never your body to transmute to the light. (Eventually, after one holds a boundary, works on himself, feels strong, has honored all that was learned from the negative, and understands that he will never unknow what he already knows, one can decide whether to "become one" with that which is of fear.)

When I was married, I couldn't share my beliefs with Jack without facing a blitz of ridicule. Now that I was an army of one, I decided to go on with what can only be described as a spiritual binge. I knew immediately where I wanted to start. Ever since I was seventeen and picked up my father's copy of *Playboy* with the interview with Elisabeth Kübler-Ross, she had been a beacon in my life. In my early thirties, I was lucky enough to meet with this great woman at her home, Healing Waters Farm, in Head Waters, Virginia. (The irony of her living on a farm with that name wasn't lost on me, either, but I chose not to mention it). I wanted to make a film on the life of this great woman, and after pulling a few strings, she finally agreed to meet with me.

I had to take two planes and a car to reach the sleepy little dot on the map. With each mile that I got closer to my destination, I became more excited and more nervous. In my years in Hollywood, I had met starlets, stars, legends, and icons. A few were geniuses. The others were either talented or just lucky. But none of them had reshaped my emotional landscape and way of thinking as had this woman I was about to meet.

Elisabeth greeted me at her front door. I tried to act sophisticated and worldly, but inside I felt like a child selling Girl Scout cookies. After twenty years, I was actually face-to-face with the major inspiration of my spiritual beliefs. Exactly how old she was at that point I couldn't say. She wasn't wearing any makeup, and the clothes she had thrown on gave little evidence that she felt meeting me was an event worth getting dolled up for. She looked to me like an ex-nun newly out of her habit. She had salt-and-pepper hair that framed a countenance that was Patricia Neal with a Swiss accent. And she appeared tired. Not the kind of tired that follows a night of festivities, but the weariness that comes when much joy has leaked out of life, and living itself has been reduced to a series of chores.

She invited me into the modest house that she had lived in for many years. She was born in Switzerland, one of triplets. Her mother dressed all three siblings identically, which wasn't unusual for the times. What did enrage tiny Elisabeth was her mother's going one step further, rubbing away any stamp of personal identity, by giving all three of them the same nickname.

As a sickly child, Elisabeth spent time in the hospital, sharing a room with a girl her own age who was in the process of dying. It was her first real glimpse at death and proved to be the cataclysmic, altering moment in her life.

While in the hospital, Elisabeth's father, the family tyrant, entered her room carrying a suitcase. He asked her what kind of a doll she wanted to keep her company as the child's long hours of confinement stretched into even longer days. Elisabeth, whose very nature was to go contrary to the prevailing tide, asked for a black one. The next day her father opened up the suitcase and rummaged his hand through it, finding a black doll that matched her desires. He took it out, but instead of handing it to her, he placed it gently on the chair just outside her reach. If she wanted it, he told her, she would have to be able to muster the strength and the will to force her sickly body to get it.

Cruel? Perhaps. Sadistic? Maybe. But for the rest of her life Elisabeth credited having to reach and strain to get that doll from the chair and into her arms as how she learned one has to fight to either live or die. Following the path that destiny had carved out for her, she became a medical doctor with psychiatry as her specialty, but it was the tightrope we all walk between this world and the next that owned her fascination.

After the war, she visited a concentration camp, where death had been at its most savage. She discovered that the children who were to be exterminated, but weren't aware of it at the time, all made various drawings on the walls of birds and butterflies and other creatures in flight, always traveling, as if from one realm to the next. She could only conclude that they instinctively knew they were going to die, and intuitively scrawled these etchings, tracing the voyage their souls would be taking.

Following her natural inclinations, Elisabeth became close to patients with cancer, prompting her to write her celebrated books on death and dying, emphasizing her belief that loved ones from the other side come to greet them when they finally cross that great divide.

She reached the pinnacle of her fame (a condition she found uncomfortable, celebrity never being a good fit to her private personality) with her renowned "five psychological stages of dying" in *On Death and Dying*.

She eventually found herself excommunicated from the medical community not just for her beliefs in life after life; she refused to rein in her contrary, searching nature. She held to the belief that her spiritual group had been disciples of Christ in an earlier life. She confessed to our mutual friend, Dr. Stan

Grof, that she was very afraid of sounding crazy.

The townspeople in that "cozy little spot" at Head Waters had no more understanding or compassion toward her and her ideas than her profession did. She told me that some of them would often crush up glass and put it in her driveway so she'd blow the tires on her car. I was going to ask her why she continued to live there, but I already knew. No matter the flood of adversity that surrounded her, the woman summoned up the will her father had honed.

There existed a profound seriousness in Elisabeth Kübler-Ross, and I remember her smiling only once that entire afternoon. It was when she related to me how she decorated her Christmas tree with little E.T. dolls. (When she told me about meeting Steven Spielberg, her face lit up from within, and her excitement was girlish and palpable.) When I left her house, there was no more talk of my making a movie about her life. It was obvious that it wasn't a subject she wanted on the screen. Although this was a blow to the producer in me, I didn't leave empty-handed. It turned out that one of her biggest gifts to me would be an introduction to her colleague, Kenneth Ring, Ph.D. At the University of Connecticut, Dr. Ring researched those who had had near-death experiences. These were all people who had, by legal standards, died, flatlined, or had an out-of-body experience and who had come back. The stories of those who had returned from the other side all had experiences that were consistent with one another. Even little children, who had no exposure to media, would return from hovering near the void with a similarly compatible story as their adult counterparts.

They all described a sense that they were intact, even if their true flesh and blood was on an operating table or beneath the wheels of a truck. With the spirit separated from the body, they all reported being imbued with a keen sense of clairvoyance. When they were revived, they could recall the exact words of those around them: the wife calling 911, the doctors operating on them. They felt as if they were being inhaled by a white light, and instead of the panic and fear that we imagine would accompany such a moment, they described their feelings as all joy, all love, and all knowing. They had shuffled off their mortal coil, if only briefly, and there was no fear, no pain, no negativity, only all ecstasy, all knowing, and all love.

Dr. Elisabeth Kübler-Ross was and would remain a hero of mine. And so it was an odd, unsettling sensation to find myself feeling sorry for someone who had been my inspiration for twenty years. But that was the emotion I carried with me as I heard the front door click behind me. She had given her life to expand people's minds, and for all her decades of work, I wanted her to live out the rest of her life as a winner.

Since her passing in 2004, I've tried to channel Elisabeth Kübler-Ross, but she's only recently come to me. I did not realize that someday, like Elisabeth and Frances, my challenge would also be to not feel crazy as I taught the ways of the other side. I too would be criticized by my colleagues, but nothing stings so much as when your own family doubts your work. Self-love comes first; all else will follow.

Chapter Sixteen

God, the Universe, and Where We Fit In

*God is seen God / In the star, in the stone,
in the flesh, in the soul and the clod.*

ROBERT BROWNING

EVEN AS A CHILD I HAD A SPECIAL AFFINITY WITH OLD PEOPLE. I felt somewhat ostracized from my contemporaries, and my parents' friends always appeared a little too impatient to really care about what was on a child's mind. Senior citizens seemed to be the only ones who really looked at me when I talked and truly cared to listen to what I had to say. The more senior the better.

Shakespeare spoke poetically about the aging process in *As You Like It*, saying that it had seven stages. It was the last stage I found to be the most interesting: "second childishness . . . sans teeth, sans eyes, sans taste, sans everything" (act ii, scene 7). In retrospect, this was only natural since I had grown up in Miami Beach, where the last stage was what surrounded me on a daily basis. An excursion to the grocery store was like a demolition derby, constantly getting slammed from carts that were bigger than the small, weak frames trying to maneuver them. Still, it was more hazardous driving to and from the market, as it appeared as if cars were piloting themselves, the shrunken drivers' heads hovering dangerously below the dashboard.

Every weekend I was taken to visit my three grandparents, who all had the good or bad luck to live well past ninety, and were by then waiting out their last years in old age homes. I remember that the halls smelled of urine, and residents were propped up in wheelchairs and left to sit unattended in their own silence. As an antidote, I memorized Jewish "Borscht Belt" jokes about the elderly. The laughs seem to deflect much of the pain I felt all around me. I became anxious about the brevity of life and afraid of the fact that someday we would all wither. Again, I found myself thinking a great deal about death, or better yet, the consequences of living a long life.

It was because of this that I felt truly in my element when, at thirteen, I became a candy striper. It gave me a needed sense of self-worth to be of whatever comfort I could to those in sickness and in death. I truly enjoyed the time I spent in the hospital. I was particularly taken with an old man who was dying in the ICU. Years later I understood that a man hooked up to

IVs and multiple machines with courses of medications and a squad of doctors and nurses, teetering on the precarious precipice of death, is expressing. His wife and children all around focused on this life actually add to the expression. Although he's expressing his "physical" in a negative way, who's to judge? His "negative physical" is expressing the "suchness" of life.

Take Mikhail Baryshnikov at the height of his ballet career (we'll forget for a moment that he smoked and drank a great deal of vodka), who primarily expressed himself through a "positive" physical aspect, not only by the magnificence of his prowess, but also by the costume fittings, rehearsal schedules, entourage responsibilities, travel, concert dates, and so on, which all added to the positive expression of this man's physicality. The "suchness" of his life was glorious. But who is to judge? Whether one chooses to express "negatively" or "positively," they are still receiving the juice of life, as they want to drink it in.

It occurred to me that we have four predominant ways of expressing ourselves: mentally, emotionally, physically, and spiritually. When I was younger, I thought the aspiration was to be balanced—not too negative, but not too positive either. Today I want to quickly learn from the "negative" and predominate my expression through the "positive."

We have all exhausted learning from the negative. I suggest we all sign up for learning through the "positive system": expansion of expression through collaboration, improvisation, connection and inspiration. Why pull in a body, relationship or work issue in order to grow? Let us begin a revolution to the "positive system".

✦   ✦   ✦

Death didn't scare me. I can only assume that somehow life's pattern of ashes to ashes made some sort of eloquent sense to me, and that I was content to let destiny rest in God's hands, even though it would take me many years to have a clear understanding of what God really is.

We're told that the universe is endless, and it certainly appears that way on a clear, star-filled night, but what exactly is "endless"?

How do we even begin to wrap our minds around a universe in which all the grains of sand on all the beaches on earth equal the stars in one galaxy alone? Or that a star we view in the evening sky has actually burned out thousands of years ago, and its light is only reaching us now. (Keep in mind that light travels at 186,282 miles per second.) The idea itself is too large and overwhelming for us to fully assign meaning to; it's ineffable.

Everything in our life has a beginning, middle, and an end, whether it's a table, a headache, or an ocean. We even take something as amorphous as time and break it down into imagined seconds and minutes until we can add them up to an hour. But that's only for our convenience; time itself is still a mystery. Why does time seem to dawdle when we're children and then gallop when we round the middle-aged stretch? Why, at the age I am now, do the seasons leapfrog over one another and another year is suddenly and forever gone?

Albert Einstein, who obviously used much more of his brain than a usual Joe, had a mental grasp of the universe that the rest of us can only attempt to comprehend. But even he, the greatest scientific mind of our time, looked upon the never-ending vastness of the cosmos and could only come to one conclusion: He believed in God, he believed in "Spinoza's God who reveals himself in the harmony of what exists."

As laypeople, some of us assume that science and spirituality are diametrically opposed. But often, as these two seemingly divergent paths of thought begin their journey by going in what appears to be opposite directions, they eventually meet. I'm told that most physicists, the poets of science, spend their working hours trying to explain the unexplainable and some of them come to the conclusion that all is governed by a divine design, an all-encompassing force that keeps the universe in perfect balance. Our world and everything outside it is too geometrically precise to be considered a random accident.

We can find faith in a myriad of ways. Some of us need churches, temples, and mosques to give structure to our belief systems. Others of us rely on a self-designed experience that does not always require community. And then there are those, like my old statistics teacher, Abby Adorney, who found it necessary to climb the steps of logic to find God. She told me that she had come to the conclusion that God must exist, because, if you took a sampling of every redwood or of every person from the tip of their finger to the end of their elbow, no matter what you're sampling, if your population was big enough, you would always have a perfect bell curve. This is true of every amoeba, tree, and person with red hair. I defy a random accident to pull off something like that.

Every culture, long before anyone ever thought to bother with recording history, believed in some type of a cohesive force, whether it was the sun, multiple deities of the rice fields and seas, or figurines of brass or stone. It's as if mankind always instinctively knew we were simply threads in a tapestry far greater than ourselves.

Children often grow up with a cookie-cutter image of God in their minds: long, white beard, dressed in what resembles a toga, with a daunting scowl stretched across his foreboding, no-nonsense countenance. Even as a child, this wasn't a vision of God I could cozy up to. We talk about his love and his blessings while we wait impatiently for a little manna from heaven to fall in our direction, yet we visualize him as the sternest of taskmasters. Like time and the universe, mankind has given him an anthropomorphized form that we can easily relate to and understand.

But are we truly supposed to be able to relate to God as if we were all members of the same golf club, much less understand him? I think it's far more likely that we have taken the Almighty and squeezed him into our own image. Across the centuries God has been twisted and turned and reshaped like clay, often used to achieve a particular culture's moral and political goals. The Almighty was turned into a spear to drive on the Crusades and a tattletale during the Salem witch hunts, while in the sixties when I was growing up, a popular slogan among hippies was "God is Dead" (my father, disdaining the way my generation dressed and wore our hair, said that if God was dead, he died from embarrassment). Fascinating phrase, "God is Dead." It takes for granted that he only exists as long as we acknowledge him.

Not only have we turned the Almighty into a replica of ourselves, but we act as if, with a snap of our fingers, we can make him come and go as we please. As with the universe and time, we seem to be only comfortable when we delude ourselves into believing that we are somehow in control. To admit that we aren't is a leap into an abyss we'd rather not venture into.

In any discussion of God, our tongue is wagging dangerously across a minefield. How each of us envisions the Almighty and chooses to relate to him is as personal as personal gets. And often even the slightest variations from our own cemented vision are viewed as nothing short of blasphemy. Wars have been waged between countries over which one has the rights to God.

As I've said earlier, I grew up in a Reform Jewish household, where God was used more like a relief pitcher, called out of the bullpen only when you were really in trouble.

Yet even as a child, my heart's gravitational pull to God was strong and unbreakable, even though I had no definite outline in my mind of what that actually might be. I knew I was a messenger.

That said, it's taken me the better part of my life to finally ascertain exactly how I do see God. The truth is, I don't. We imagine God as an external force, enveloping us like a tent, but is that entirely accurate? When we pray, and there's a true spiritual connection, don't we feel God inside us? The very act of prayer itself is a spiritual conversation. Not the kind of prayers we learn by rote as children that roll off our tongues with no thought or heart having to be involved, but rather those silent prayers that emanate from so deep within us we can feel them rattling the emptiness inside us as they rise. And when we do connect with God on a purely spiritual level, we can actually feel the energy filling us. I don't see God, but I feel his presence within me.

As I've noted, Einstein believed in a Divine Being. He is, for me, a perfect example of the way in which God exists. How, exactly, did Einstein, only in his thirties and having failed math in school, peer out into the universe and come up with the theory of relativity? Thomas Edison, that other great mind occupying the same time period, described genius as "one percent inspiration and ninety-nine percent perspiration." It's that one percent that changes civilizations and alters our perception of the universe. And it's that one percent of Divine inspiration that I believe to be God.

Edison was asked in an interview what he thought of Einstein's theory, and the great inventor replied that he didn't think anything of it, "Because I don't understand it." Edison was either being extremely modest, or he truly didn't understand it.

I tend to believe that the latter was true. Genius is usually pin-pointed to one specific area, and I doubt whether Mozart or Shakespeare or Van Gogh, geniuses all, would have been able to make heads or tails of the way Einstein's mind had reshaped our universe. Does this make Einstein a greater genius than all those other geniuses? I would say no, understanding that every genius has his own particular sandbox to play in.

Einstein's mind burrowed further and deeper into the questions of the universe than any other, while Shakespeare's genius used words to dissect every emotion beating inside the human heart. But what was it that was in Shakespeare that allowed him to create *Hamlet* and Mozart to write *Don Giovanni*? If it came out of the 99 percent perspiration then, hell, I could have written them. With that not being the case, it leaves us with that one percent of inspiration, that unseen spark of creativity that magically bursts into flame. Where does it come from, and what allows it to suddenly ignite?

Irving Berlin is acknowledged to have been our greatest composer of popular music. (When Jerome Kern was asked what place his contemporary occupied in music, Kern succinctly replied, "Irving Berlin has no place in American music. He is American music.") The width and breadth of his brilliance is overwhelming viewed from any angle, but made even more staggering when we consider that Berlin only had a fifth grade education and needed someone else to jot down his compositions, transferring his genius into musical notes on the page (compositions that became tent poles of the American psyche, including

"White Christmas," "God Bless America," and "Easter Parade").

Berlin's popularity was so great and the reason for his genius so mystifying that the usual happened—a rumor spread around Tin Pan Alley that he didn't actually write his songs, but they were composed by a "little colored boy who resided in Berlin's piano." Shakespeare's reputation has also gone through its tarnishing by envy. The Bard, though having been schooled, didn't possess an Oxford-caliber education, and many scholars have come to believe he didn't have the knowledge to be the creator of such masterworks, handing the credit over to his contemporary, Christopher Marlowe, instead. Interesting speculation, but with one gigantic loophole: If this is so, why didn't Marlowe sign his real name to *Hamlet* and *Othello* instead of giving the credit to some Elizabethan hack? It only makes sense that if he had actually been the author of Shakespeare's work, he'd want those things on his résumé.

Genius can pop up anywhere, like dandelions, but we want a reason for it, as if we could reduce it to a formula that we could follow and thereby control. But there is no map that will lead us to creation. Then where does it come from, that split second when we suddenly see something we had never seen before, and, in some cases, that the world has never seen before? To me, God is the moment of creation, the moment of enlightenment. All is God. God is All.

There's been a lot of educated guesswork that has gone into trying to comprehend how the universe was created. One of the most popular of these is the big bang theory, which holds that all matter in the universe had once been one and then exploded into the quadrillion of bits and pieces that make up all the stars and planets in our universes. What this theory can't explain is how this tremendous ball of everything came into existence in the first place and what made it blow apart. There is no explanation for what ignited the spark, as there is no explanation for what ignites creativity. To me, that spark is God.

This is what I mean when I say that God is inside us—not just in the ten trillion cells that make up the human body, but the empty space that surrounds it. We're taught that we can only get to God by going through religion, turning our particular faith into a sort of middleman or road map. Unfortunately, when we exit the doors of our place of worship, that's often the last we think of God until the following week.

How different our attitude becomes when we accept the gift of God being inside us, sparking the fuse of inspiration that can lead us to altering the course of our lives. God is the masterful compilation of all that is. It is the space between what has been and what is coming. It is the Divine spark of what is unfurled energy and lessons not yet learned.

Just as my mother and I came into mutual forgiveness and deepened the connection as equals, could we do this with God? What if we could come from a more mature acceptance that we must cocreate our destiny with a friend who wanted us to attain all that we design for ourselves? Wouldn't we have to look very carefully at what is ours? Then the words "Higher Power" take on a new meaning. We are ONE. We are ALL. We are the fabric with which we have all that is ours. Heady, yeah. But what if?

What if we are just as we make ourselves? Our thought patterns, our design is exactly as—we eventually come to realize—we wanted all along. Why wait for a "life review" to see yourself as love? Because there is no death, there is no judgment for *anything* you have done. You find self-love from all that you are: *expression*. So help create all that you express *now*. See yourself as capable of attaining all that you have and are and more. See yourself as being the best you. You are a creator. God is your copilot, so *fly high*.

Rush to make yourself all that you are, and see yourself in control. Do not give rise to a lower or weaker position. Use your experience to learn what is yours to do. Seek counsel from advisors here and on alternate planes to give you insight into the glorious partnership we all have. There is no time like the present. Enjoy it all. Sit back and *love*. Sudden flashes of insight that apply to our work, our marriage, or ourselves allow us to take one step further in living the lives we desire and are the very essence of God, I believe.

When my life reached its lowest ebb, when my husband, friends, and, finally, my career, evaporated, I suddenly knew what I wanted to do with the rest of my time here on earth. God lit up another avenue to pursue, allowing me to walk toward a life I believe had always been waiting for me.

I was in preparation to be a messenger.

Chapter Seventeen

My Second Act

*There are no elements so diverse that they
cannot be joined in the heart of a man.*

JEAN GIRAUDOUX

IN ITS YOUTH, WHEN TELEVISION WAS FLICKERING BLACK-
AND-WHITE and tinfoil wrapped around rabbit ears was the
difference between clarity and static, one of the shows that
local stations liked to broadcast to fill airtime was a game show
called *Bowling for Dollars* (the title tells you everything you need
to know).

As a child I watched it with an almost religious fervor usually
reserved for only the maddest of zealots, although I don't
remember caring about who won or the amount of money that

would be his after the tournament was over. The reason for my dedicated viewing was to watch the bowling ball as it barreled down the lane before crashing into the awaiting still life of pins. What captured my complete attention, the moment that never failed to leave me mystified, was when the ball, rolling head-long toward the gutter, seemed to magically change direction and aim itself directly toward the center pin.

I thought about that bowling ball many years later when I had a similar moment and had to decide to change course. At an age when most women are deciding whether to let their hair go gray or splash it with color from a tube, I bought a book bag and enrolled in night school at Ryokan College. As I expected, I was one of the oldest bowling pins there. By day I still busied myself rolling the boulder uphill trying to get a film, any film, made, while my evenings were given over to school and my children.

It immediately felt right, like slipping on your most com-fortable pair of shoes. School ignited a spark in me, and I found myself excited again. Enthusiastic. Passionate. And always just a little nervous, but in that good way that makes you try a little harder to succeed. It wasn't long before I willingly shed the illu-sion of making movies and threw myself completely into my new career goal. Even as I was filling dozens of spiral notebooks in a classroom, my mind was already leapfrogging ahead of itself, searching for the missing, vital piece in most conven-tional therapy that's necessary to give patients the emotionally rich, fulfilling life that had always managed to elude them.

I followed this belief when it came time to do my dissertation. Through a case study, I organized principles for a new form of analysis based on intuition. It was visibly obvious that most patients have a hunger and a thirst for definitions to ideas that they had previously felt were regarded as "crazy." They need a deeper understanding of their intuition, and when found, they revel in the discovery of their own unique connection to their God-self.

It was at this point when my two lives met and mingled, and I suddenly realized I could pour everything I had learned from my past career into the one I was now dedicated to forging.

Show business is a stew where genius and mediocrity coexist in the same pot. The difference is that the most abundantly talented may also be the ones who feel the most like frauds. (Creativity is a right-brain activity. Most creative, visio-spatial, and musical people are right-brain dominant. Negative emotions also reside in the right brain.)

Success in any form takes enormous work and a laserlike concentration, and if you're a bee and have only one job to do in order to keep the hive buzzing, that's fine. As human beings, we're capable of a rainbow of diverse achievements. But even the greatest of jugglers can toss one too many balls in the air. Anyone strenuously climbing the ladder to get to his goal doesn't seem to have the time, energy, or necessary inclination to pour into other areas of his life. And so everything else is put on hold, while he soothes himself by subconsciously believing that they'll remain frozen in time like statues until he can eventually clear off his desk and circle his calendar. His children will remain young and adoring, and his wife will remain patient, accepting, and in love until he can get back to them. And the other parts of himself, well, he'll take care of them someday, too.

I knew these go-getters well. They were my friends and coworkers, many of them immensely talented, bright, and charming. And they were empty inside. Somewhere along the way to fame and fortune, they had lost the emotional and spiritual core that we all need to sustain us. And that, I realized, was the missing piece. Did they have a purpose, a passion, a love for something larger than their own ego?

For me, spirituality is the ability to be awed through your connection to creation, to know your purpose, and to be of service—all to find faith, hope, and inner peace. This was at the very heart of what I call "soul communion." I knew that, on its face, this sounded esoteric and mystical, but I also realized that it was already threaded into the fabric of most people's lives.

After all, who hasn't prayed to a loved one who has died, talked to them, and asked them for emotional and spiritual guidance? Our stumbling block is that we talk, say a quick "Amen," and never wait around to listen.

Soul communion is teaching ourselves how to wait around and listen. We believe in the spiritual realm, yet at the same time we shut ourselves off from it. We pray for help and then don't allow it to help us. Irony doesn't get more self-defeating. When we look at a child with a particular gift, whether for science, art, math, or music, we feel it's a duty that he fosters that talent, allowing it the wings to soar. That consciousness is God's gift to us, and it's our responsibility to cultivate it.

To make spiritual contact with our guidance realm, we have to fit ourselves into that same emotional mode. (To put it more simply: relax.) We have to learn to break our "loner." That's the unyielding bit of James Dean in all of us that pushes against authority. Not a bad thing, as it's necessary to help each of us develop our personality and understand our own uniqueness, allowing us to form our own sovereign structure. But once our personalities have been fully developed and ingrained, we can relax our stance and break our loner, finally comfortable enough within ourselves to feel free to ask for help, and allow it to come to us from all realms and all dimensions that operate from love and light.

Finding a way to combine psychology with spirituality was my new goal, my all-consuming passion. In order to receive my doctoral degree, I needed a certain amount of practical, supervised patient hours. I went on a job interview with Richard Rogg at Promises Malibu. As I nervously got ready, giving myself a final once-over before leaving my house, I flashed back on that young woman all those years ago who was dressing to go for her first interview at Creative Artists Agency. I was naturally older, and certainly not as wide-eyed.

The big difference between me and that girl, I realized, was that she was all starry-eyed about what she wanted to accomplish, while I was more concerned with what I could accomplish for others. I remember smiling as I thought to myself, *I may not be as cute and sexy as that other girl, but wisdom isn't a bad compensation.*

In the middle of my interview with Richard, he happened to mention that he had some empty office space on the corner of Pacific Coast Highway and Sunset Boulevard. Without a thought, I blurted out that I had a dream to start a holistic, psychological, spiritual institute. I hadn't even gotten my doctoral degree yet, and here I was sharing my dreams. I waited for Richard to respond with that chilly glare of professional condescension I had come to know so well from my days working with Mike Ovitz. If it appeared, I didn't have time to see it.

Suddenly everything went white. My eyes were not only taking in Richard's face, but also a pouring in of white light. (This phenomenon is known in 12-step recovery groups by the punchy title, "a God shot.") I could only explain the sudden flash as being God and guidance's cheering punctuation to go for it!

I knew at that moment that this was my calling. Of course, answering that call isn't always that easy, but I knew that somehow I would combine the producing and agenting skills I had sharpened over the years to get it done. Nothing is for naught. My biggest obstacle was a financial one. I didn't have any money. I was in school siphoning off the last of my reserves, and there was no way a new, unlicensed intern would be able to earn the money necessary to found and fund an institute. Still, I refused to be deterred. To the best of my knowledge, no one has ever achieved anything far-reaching without putting on blinders first. Whenever I consulted my guidance, I heard, "trust."

The idea continued to grow as my finances continued to

shrink. It was starting to appear as if the impossible was truly that. It was then that I got the phone call telling me my eighty-five-year-old aunt Jeanne had died. Her soul had finally severed the last string holding it to this world. I was relieved for this dear, sad woman, who had been only marking time on this earth since her son Billy died at age twenty-six from drug abuse.

Whatever dim flame had flickered inside her at the end of her days loved me with a timing that was beyond her consciousness. Aunt Jeanne had left me an inheritance of half of her house. I now had the seed money to begin turning my impossible dream into a reality. Some would call this serendipity, as if we inadvertently step haphazardly into good fortune the same way we would a gopher hole. I prefer to believe that there are unbreakable, albeit invisible strings being pulled that often give our lives direction and purpose. Addiction had killed my aunt's son, and now I would use the money she'd left me to stop it from destroying other families.

It was a distant dream that reality continually reminded me was far beyond my grasp, often shrouded over by sleepless nights and the constant hammering of money worries. But even during the worst of times, the dark clouds covering my skies seemed to separate just enough for me to see a thin sliver of hope peeking out at me from the distance. With that I prayed, and the name of my dream came: Moonview.

Moonview, a sanctuary of calm and order in a world of chaos, pressure, and fear. I called it Moonview, because the moon reflects the sun's light. Since the beginning of time, humanity has been afraid of the night, the unseen, and excited by the first crack of morning light. Our night, our most covert nature, our emotions that crave illumination . . . Moonview. The moon is feminine, that part of us that intuits and receives. To view is masculine, the first action before growth. In Chinese calligraphy, when you put the sun and the moon together, they light up the world toward enlightenment.

Chapter Eighteen

Jerry

Wounds cannot be cured without searching.

FRANCIS BACON

I APPROACHED THE CREATION OF MOONVIEW like a true zealot, and I brought my new partners, Terry Egan, M.D., and Stephen Sideroff, Ph.D., together to work on what was fast becoming a new paradigm for psychological healing. My plans for a holistic mental health institute were speedily mushrooming from a dream into an obsession. As I quickly learned, the difference between a dream and an obsession is that a good obsession costs one hell of a lot more money. We worked for seven years, sharing our patients, bringing in pilot patients, and researching different constellations of multiple treatments, all in a concentrated effort to quicken traditional courses of healing.

I became keenly aware of the landscape of my field: Reimbursements for psychiatric, psychological, and holistic services are drastically and inhumanely insufficient. The bulk of the research and money goes for clinical trials on the latest new drug, not applications of new, exciting combinations of treatments where the team shares results and inspires refinement of the newly innovated methodologies. So even if you can get talk therapy covered on your insurance, it can be a very slow process.

People are all unique in the way they process information; some specialize in being auditory, while others process information visually, analytically, or kinesthetically). Where people "hold" their trauma (body, thoughts, reactions) is different for everyone. Each one of us is different in expressing difficult internal states or how they take us over and when we are stressed. One practitioner or one style of healing does not adequately address an individual's comprehensive needs. And what's more, how is that either time- or cost-effective?

My partners and I came together to design a new model of healing. We wanted to do research on individual case studies to prove our understanding of holistic healing. First, we would need to have a thorough assessment that included much more than a typical psych assessment. We would administer a quantitative electroencephalography (QEEG) and look at nineteen placements on the brain. The results of the QEEG assessment would be compared to normative data. We would look for

either under- or overactivation of the brain and be able to deter-
mine cites to train. By training the brain to shift out of its old
patterns we would enhance brain flexibility which facilitates
cognitive flexibility and brain function.

We would study attachment strategies in family of origin as
well as current communication styles, trauma memory in both
the nervous system and the body, stress and anxiety levels, and
so on. The best part is that each evaluation and program would
be customized by a team that "think tanks" on each case every
day. We knew that we were sitting on top of a "winner."

As we continued to climb toward our therapeutic goal, I
couldn't help but notice that the financial ground I was standing on was fast becoming a sinkhole, threatening to swallow
me and everything I owned. The inheritance from my aunt
Jeanne had long been spent, and I continued to stoke the fire
of my compulsion by personally investing my savings. Now I
stood on the brink of mortgaging my house.

I would have preferred concentrating on my dream rather
than the multiple land mines along the way, but sleepless nights
seem to be reserved for worry and panic. Yet each time I asked
my God-self to scatter a few breadcrumbs to lead me out of the
forest I was in, I heard "Trust." I trusted, but it did nothing to
assuage my fears. Lying in bed at three in the morning I felt like
one of those greyhounds chasing a mechanical rabbit round
and round a racetrack. The goal is always just a little out of
reach.

It's during those black hours late at night, when the rest of the world seems contentedly asleep, when you glance back in memory to the choices you've made and the beautifully paved roads you were too stubborn to take. Lying to yourself is like cheating at solitaire; it's so damned tempting, and who's going to know? Now here I was, asking my heart what I would have done differently. Self-honesty is at its most unadorned in the early hours, as it's tough to lie to yourself at three in the morning. As precarious as my financial state was and as threadbare as my nerves were becoming, I realized that even if given the opportunity, I wouldn't change anything. When I understood that, all that was left to me was to pour all my faith into the dream I was hoping to make real. And as St. Augustine so succinctly put it, "Faith is to believe what we do not see; the reward of this faith is to see what we believe." I finally fell asleep, hoping that St. Augustine knew what he was talking about.

It was the best sleep I'd had in months, and when I woke up I was both refreshed and energized. Unfortunately, I was just as broke and Moonview was still only penciled plans on a drawing board. But what had changed was my attitude. What I'd previously viewed as a swirling cyclone of financial disaster I now embraced with a newly found excitement.

What I needed was a way to get our research out and financially backed. My trusted partner and medical director, Terry Eagan, suggested I go directly to Gerald "Jerry" Levin, who had announced his retirement as CEO from that media behemoth Time Warner. I didn't know Levin and he certainly didn't know me, but he stated that he wanted to be a social activist. I hoped that might include being on the board of Moonview. After all, he certainly had a way to get the research out, and the mission was to have a privileged few sponsor a mental/spiritual revolution.

It was a wonderful idea, and I hated it immediately. Instinctively the idea felt right, but fund-raising has never been my strongest muscle, and even when I collected for the United Nations Children's Fund (UNICEF) on Halloween as a child, I felt a little hesitant. Putting my palm out for money brought back the memory of asking my father for my allowance during the austerity program days. My dad's face would twist into a pained look that said, "I wish I could, but I can't." Since then I've found it far less humiliating to just keep my hands in my pockets.

As much as I tried to dodge it, my instinct told me that Terry was right. And instinct is like a peptic ulcer; try to ignore it and you're only heading for trouble. I called Levin directly—and he picked up the phone. I cannot overstate how unusual this was. It was a cold call. After pursuing business titans for twenty years, I'd learned from experience that they rarely take cold calls from anyone. Heck, they seldom take calls from people they do know. (Your name is usually jotted down on a list by a secretary, and you're promised you'll be gotten back to. I wouldn't suggest anyone hold their breath while waiting for their phone to ring.)

What I didn't know at the time was that the man on the other end of the phone was also at the end of his rope. Levin was one of those rare men standing atop the highest mountain peak who had never planned on going mountain climbing in the first place. In college he had pictured himself in a corduroy jacket

standing in front of a classroom, pointing out the intricate relationships that Dostoyevsky had surgically woven through the
pages of *The Brothers Karamazov*. At night he would be ensconced
in a tiny den until the wee hours, pouring his heart into the
writing of his own novel. This was his "road not taken."

Whether he wanted it or not, Jerry had a genius for commerce, and his artistic nature curled up like an old dog in front
of a fireplace while his business acumen took him to the top.
But by the time he got there, he was alone. Only one of two
things can happen to a visionary working in the bubble of big
business: he either gets kicked upstairs or kicked out the door.
Jerry took the stairs.

It was the era when corporations merged more often than
rabbits, and Jerry was instrumental in birthing HBO, the marriage of Time Inc. with Warner Communications, buying CNN
and brokering the consolidation of AOL and Time Warner to
form the world's biggest media conglomerate. With that single
stroke, his business acumen was immediately regarded to be the
most far-reaching in the high-stakes world of commerce. The
man who had only a few years earlier seen his destiny as scribbling out novels in a dank attic was suddenly thrust center stage
as the golden boy of big business.

All conglomerates, no matter how big or how successful, are
embedded with a tapeworm, forcing them to keep eating.
Although cable television appeared as if its best days were
behind it, Jerry insisted on paying 12 billion dollars to purchase
and make a meal of Ted Turner's cable networks. This dubious

decision proved brilliant, adding wattage to Levin's already blinding luster.

He had money, power, and the fawning respect of the entire business community. He stood alone on the mountaintop. And, thanks to his vision, the mountain continued to get bigger and bigger. The trouble with mountaintops is that there's not much oxygen up there. You can start hallucinating and begin to believe the juicy compliments people are slathering you with are both heartfelt and actually true.

Anyone who has read Shakespeare's towering tragedy *King Lear* has an inkling of what happened next. Because there's only room for one on a mountaintop, Jerry's relationship with his wife began unspooling, finally settling into the well-worn hammock of being a marriage of inconvenience. They were living in separate residences and disaggregating their finances. (Obviously there were a thousand other reasons, as with my own marriage to Jack, but when a porcupine throws its quills, it's impossible to know which is the fatal one.)

In the best of circumstances, real friends are as rare as four-leaf clovers. The more powerful you are, the more sycophants crowd around you, smiling and nodding and laughing on cue, but true friends are scarce. Jerry had 90,000 people working under him, and he was becoming more and more isolated. At the same time, he learned that his old college roommate was dying of stomach cancer. Jerry was losing the only friend who had known and remembered the real man underneath the gated exterior.

Then, as the skyrocket of his career hit its zenith, the bottom
fell out of his life, leaving him with nothing to believe in or
hold on to. In 1997 Jerry's son, Jonathan, was a schoolteacher
in the Bronx. He had specifically chosen to work in that blackboard jungle because he truly believed that no child was
beyond redemption. He was his father's pride and prize, having
chosen to travel the road his father had only dreamed about.
Jon was robbed at gunpoint of his ATM card and code by one
of his ex-students who he had tried to help. The grisly trans-
action was concluded when he shot Jon through the head,
killing him instantly.

Jonathan's senseless death sent shock waves through the
entire educational system. Many universities began to take on
the task of informing young educators just how to work in
inner-city schools. Jon's chosen avenue in reaching his students
was through media, and now media centers were being added
to curriculums and campuses in his name. Jon's murder had
inflamed education for change.

And if Jerry's heart took comfort in this, it didn't stop the
change that had taken place inside him. The most excruciating
pain anyone can suffer, the kind that refuses to ever go away, is
the loss of a child. There are no bandages or remedies, and it's
the one wound that time cannot heal. In a flash his life had lost
all meaning and all direction. He had no spiritual well to drink
from, so he took the only path he knew, the only path still open
to him, and threw himself into his work.

But it just wasn't working anymore. Whatever emotional center Jerry had managed to cobble together for himself over the years had crumbled under devastation and torment. Jon and Jerry shared the same birthday. They had a love and ease with each other that defied words. His boy was gone. The summa cum laude titan had no knowledge or advisor to resolve his agony. He took refuge in the comfortable and the known, working harder and longer hours, allowing the business, a business he never wanted to be in, to numb his senses against the pain. Jerry made an unspoken, unconscious pact to replace his anguish with internal rage and external arrogance, both of which covered the deep, dark pool of hopelessness and regret.

Las Vegas stays in business on the assumption that human nature will keep a gambler at the dice table for one roll too many. This is especially true when that lucky gambler comes to believe that he's gold-plated and invincible. Jerry was playing the odds, and they were certainly in his favor. Keeping one eye on the future, he believed the Internet was the new frontier that had only begun to be explored, its riches still waiting to be mined.

With the board signing on to his new venture, Jerry traded away a giant 55 percent of Time Warner stock in exchange for America Online. On paper the deal was as shrewd and brilliant as any he had maneuvered. But timing is everything, and his timing, which had once been impeccable, now failed him. It was the beginning of the new millennium, right before the fantasy of all the endless wealth the Internet would provide suddenly crashed and burned.

It proved to be a gargantuan misstep, costing Time Warner an estimated 200 billion dollars, and all the grateful stockholders who had once fawned over him now got out their torches and pitchforks. They believed their golden boy was just another greedy CEO whose wallet only grew heftier as "the little people" saw their money and dreams suddenly evaporate.

What they didn't know, and what Jerry refused to broadcast, was that he financially refused to save himself, allowing the tidal wave he had set in motion to hit him the hardest.

And then came the final straw. It seems there's always a final straw just waiting in the wings. Jerry's occurred a few days after 9/11, a day that left New Yorkers, as well as the rest of the country, disbelieving and shattered. But not, it would seem, quite everyone. His associates at AOL–Time Warner pushed him to hold a board meeting that had already been scheduled. Jerry refused, perhaps adding a handful of epithets for color, but at that moment he knew it was over. He didn't know the life he wanted, but it was very clear to him that his present life was one he could no longer live.

After Jon's death, Jerry had thrown himself into work at a blistering pace in a failed attempt to numb his grief. As people so often do, he tried to bury his pain rather than confront it.

But the morning of 9/11 reactivated all of the unresolved trauma that he had been refusing to deal with honestly. He identified with all the families who were drowning in shock and despair just from sending a loved one off to work that morning. His son's death and his inability to cope with it had twisted

Jerry into someone spiteful and bitter. He beat his body down with excruciating hours, stilled his emotions by adding girder to his gate, and overrode others with blinding flashes of impatience and arrogance.

The devastation of 9/11 was his personal ground zero at a core level. All the pain came flooding back, but this time he found it impossible to hold it at bay. He understood subconsciously that Jon's death could not be in vain, and the truest way for him to honor his son was to do something he would never have done for himself: he had to change.

Gerald Levin resigned as CEO of AOL–Time Warner as 2001 folded itself into the following year. Before the scepter of power was officially passed, Jerry was given a smaller office with a telephone that never rang where he could uncomfortably wait out the remainder of his time. And that was where he was temporarily ensconced when he uncharacteristically picked up the phone to speak to me.

Chapter Nineteen

You Never See the Lightning Coming

Love, with very young people, is a heartless business.
We drink at that age from thirst, or to get drunk;
it is only later in life that we occupy ourselves
with the individuality of our wine.

ISAK DINESEN

I INTRODUCED MYSELF WITH MY NEW TITLE AND OLD NAME, Dr. Laurie Perlman. My moniker certainly made me sound important enough to talk to, as even retiring CEOs always have one doctor or another calling them with their latest cholesterol results. The moment I got Jerry on the line, I catapulted into my pitch for Moonview, my desire for his support, and my hopes of adding his name to the board. (I had no way of knowing at the time the microscopic regard in which he currently held "boards.")

Although I was quite sure he was only half listening, he agreed to meet with me. I was both disbelieving and thrilled that he would squeeze us into his schedule, not realizing that at that moment his schedule was more open than the Grand Canyon. In a whoosh of excitement, I poured all my hopes and dreams for Moonview into a tidy prospectus and, along with Terry Eagan, quickly hopped a plane to New York. (I know that's usually just an expression, but I was so thrilled I actually did hop.)

Arming myself with as much information as possible before that first meeting, I began sifting through articles about the man whose support I desperately needed to turn Moonview into a reality. It was only then that I learned about the details of the tragic circumstances under which he had lost his son, Jonathan.

I thought it might be helpful if I could channel Jonathan before meeting Jerry, though channeling is a two-way street, and unless that soul on the other side wants to make contact, the entire endeavor becomes as fruitless as attempting to talk to a real person when you call your cable company.

That night I was surprised at how quickly Jon came to me, almost as if he had been impatiently waiting for someone to reach out to him. He told me that his father was in an unhappy marriage. It was a mental marriage, with no intimacy. (Only later did I discover that the marriage Jerry was currently in was not with Jon's mother.) He also told me that the brutality of his murder blew open his father's heart, which had grown cold and callous over the years of business. I believed Jon was preparing me for the meeting. The rest of the night I slept fitfully, wondering about the man I would be meeting with in the morning. Who was this business titan whose son seemed so desperate to help from the other side?

I had never met Jerry, although I realized it was more than possible that we may have attended some of the same premieres or industry parties. Maybe we nodded, perhaps even exchanged a passing smile, but our twains wouldn't have gone so far as to actually meet. He would have been clustered on the business side of the room, where deals were discussed and mergers mentioned. I would have gravitated toward the production executives or the writers, actors, and directors who thought a party was for chatter and laughter and breaking from your shell like a newly born chick.

Before our all-important meeting with Jerry in his office at 75 Rockefeller Center, Terry and I had an early breakfast at the Plaza, but we were too nervous to do more than just play with the oatmeal we had ordered. Although we still had time to kill, after sipping our coffee as slowly as possible, we knew we couldn't stay there any longer without being ticketed for loitering.

Meandering down Fifth Avenue we came upon St. Patrick's Cathedral, situated directly opposite our destination. Both of us have relaxed religious practices, although Terry is the son of a Southern Baptist minister. We quickly climbed the steps into Manhattan's religious landmark and began lighting every candle we could get our hands on. I have a feeling that God doesn't bother to card people before listening to their prayers. After filling St. Patrick's with prayer and smoke, Terry and I crossed Fifth Avenue and headed for the most important meeting of our lives.

Moments later Terry and I were in the elevator climbing to the top of Manhattan's skyline to meet Jerry in his button-downed corporate world. I would have asked myself what the hell I thought I was doing, but the truth is, I suddenly became so excited that even my thoughts stuttered.

At first sight Jerry is an imposing figure, lean and opaque and throwing a large shadow, with every business deal he has ever transacted etched somewhere on his face. But what I felt immediately was the protective wall that surrounded him, which I could only assume he had erected brick by painful brick. And in that instant I wasn't nervous anymore. Like Androcles confronting the lion for the first time, I found him to be wounded and silently suffering. (Jon's words had helped.)

The years I had spent in the foxhole of CAA as an agent had honed my powers of persuasion to a sharp point, and I had become particularly adept at reading the emotions of the individual sitting opposite me. But as I talked, Jerry remained a polite, well-mannered blank page, giving me no overt insights or clues as to what he was feeling, a necessary skill for both CEOs and high-stakes poker players. Through the years I'd learned to recognize when a meeting was over, and I could usually tell which way the wind was blowing. But now the air remained perfectly still. The meeting was over in one hour, and I had no idea whether anything I had said had registered with the man we had flown cross-country to meet.

As Terry and I were leaving the office, I suddenly heard Jon's voice, "Hug him, hug him." Having spent years in show business I was well versed in touchy-feely, which is the ability to show affection to someone you don't know and wouldn't recognize if you passed them on the street the next day. It was definitely not something I felt comfortable doing or deemed appropriate, but having promised myself to always listen to and follow the guidance realm, I didn't feel I had much to say in the matter.

With my feet almost out the door, I quickly did a U-turn and threw my arms around Jerry. Then, not wanting to stick around to see his expression, I got the hell out of there. But I did take a long look at the shock pasted on Terry's face as we took the elevator back down to earth. "You hugged him," he kept repeating, unable to quite believe what he knew he had just seen. "That man's depressed," Terry said when he finally got back his mental bearings. "We should get him flowers."

I stopped at a nearby florist. I plucked raspberry ranunculus, magenta peonies, lemon calla lilies, and lime green spider mums. I asked for something, "a little better than breathtaking." The woman behind the counter came up with a floral masterpiece, with brighter colors than even Monet knew existed. She handed me the little card to write my message. With pen in hand I stood like stone, realizing I didn't have a message. And then I heard Jon's voice again, piping into me as clearly and as declaratively as before. "Write 'You're wonderful,'" he instructed me. It was a little much, I thought, but I did as I was told. What the hell? At least I didn't have to be in his office when he read it. I signed Terry and my full names, including our degree initials, attempting to keep it as professional as I could, although any type of floral arrangement seems a little outside the well-structured box of big business.

Jerry called the next day to thank me, and I could tell by the tone of his voice that he really meant it. Only then did I realize that when you're the outgoing CEO of a giant conglomerate, there aren't too many flowers coming your way. Terry and I flew back to Los Angeles, where I concerned myself with the dimming rainbow of hopes I had funneled into Moonview, as well as all the money I had drained from my bank account. At night I tossed and turned more than I slept, spending hours staring up at the ceiling and wondering just how much longer I could afford for that ceiling to be over me.

Two weeks later I was walking my dog along the early morning strip of beach, hoping the salt air would clear my mind. I tried not to think of anything, for at this point almost everything that popped into my head was depressing. And then I heard Jon's voice. "Call him," he said. "It's 6:30 in the morning!" I said. Jon trumped with, "It's 9:30 in New York." I didn't want to. There was no point, I told myself. I was quite positive that Jerry had forgotten both me and Moonview the moment I left his office. Even when I was an agent, I was never very good at being pushy.

Every bone in my body resisted making that call, but when both my guide and God-self insist, I don't argue. I made myself pick up the phone and dial, hoping he'd be in one of those meetings all executives seem to be in when they don't want to talk to you. But once again I got through to him directly. I had hoped I would think of something clever to say; one of those great things that pop into your head at the last second and save you, like a parachute opening right before you hit the ground.

Unfortunately, my mental parachute remained as tangled as my tongue. Short on any form of chitchat, I gave him a brief status report about a new investor lunch for Moonview. After that it seemed I had nothing to say to Jerry, and he certainly had nothing to say to me. After being an agent for a decade, I would have hoped my mouth knew enough to keep talking even after my brain had stopped participating, but my usual conversational skills were short-circuited. My guide and God-self waited as the silence grew deeper and warmer, and I quite suddenly had perfect faith that all was right. Although no words were being spoken, neither one of us could manage to utter good-bye. Finally I heard myself say, "You realize neither of us can hang up. We must have work to do together." Jerry had no response, "Uh-uh," and like a tennis match where the ball has gone dead, we finally let our wordless conversation mercifully conclude.

I did not wonder why Jon had insisted I call his father. (If one has had a sense of humor in this realm, they carry it with them to the next. Humor is as much a part of one's spirit as any emotion, and from all I have since heard, Jon's sense of humor and appreciation of timing was second to none.) But Jon's purpose ran deeper than that. His goal was to keep my line of communication with his father open after I had already assumed it had closed.

And it was that phone call that led, a few months later, to Terry and me returning to Manhattan to have breakfast with Jerry in Time Warner's private dining room at 75 Rock. Up until then Jerry had been all business, without allowing us so much as a glimmer of his true emotions. But on this day, after half-heartedly eating only a few bites of his berries and cereal, he abruptly shifted the conversation to his old college roommate who was currently wasting away from stomach cancer. It was as if Jerry couldn't hold the pain by himself any longer, and the wall he had been building around himself for so many years finally began to crack from the pressure.

It was a business breakfast that suddenly had nothing to do with business, but rather the common denominator of pain and loss that binds all of us together. Why this very private man had chosen me to discuss this with, I could only guess at, but I imagine he had heard enough about my hopes for Moonview to know where my heart was. Jerry listened intently as I told him of the work of Elisabeth Kübler-Ross, and if it didn't give him relief from his suffering, it did seem to offer some sort of temporary respite.

After breakfast Jerry motioned Terry to the window. He wanted to show Terry a concert-size screen of the U.S. Open's live feed and bleachers erected on the Rockfeller Center yard. Wanting to see too, I walked behind Jerry, but a bolt of invisible electricity shocked me so hard, I literally flew backward into the wall. I could barely stand up. I was weak in the knees. The current that ran through me went unnoticed by Jerry and Terry. I quietly and quickly pulled myself together the best I could.

Well, Jon sure as hell got my attention.

My attention was held long after I returned to Los Angeles. The truth is I couldn't stop thinking about Jerry, and I couldn't stop wondering why I couldn't stop thinking about him. No matter where I was or what I was doing, he was always orbiting my thoughts. I hadn't thought I was attracted to him, priding myself on the parsing of the professional and the personal, but now I felt like a schoolgirl scribbling little hearts all over her geometry notebook. Truth too, he wasn't my type. He was married, depressed, and walled up. (Not that "my type" had, in the end, ever proven to be my type.)

What made this particularly awkward was that I had been on-again, off-again with someone for two years. (Even when he was on I wished he'd get off.) Neither one of us was noticeably swept off our feet, and though I called it a love affair, it was really more like a "Are you as lonely as I am?" affair.

I came back to Los Angeles with enormous confusion. I curled up in my bedroom to have a one-on-one with God. First, as with any good invocation, I had to set the mood. In the glow of candles, I closed my eyes, calmed my breathing, and prayed:

"Dear God, please give me a sneak preview of my future." Suddenly (as had happened only once before during the *Roger Rabbit* screening), a Kodak perfect snapshot of Jerry in a cardigan standing in a beach house kitchen with grandbabies crawling on the floor flashed in my mind. I panicked; first the electrical charge from Jon and now another confirmation directly from God. Both gratitude and panic surged.

Finding myself unable to unscramble my own feelings, I put in an emergency call to a girlfriend who was also one of the best intuitives I knew. I told her of my emotional dilemma and she calmly asked for Jerry's date of birth. I told her, and I remember her reply word for word:

"Are you sitting down? You were both married before. You will blow him open spiritually, and he will teach you responsibility in business, and together you'll bring a new love into the world."

No pressure there. This was a hefty bit of information to try and take in, as up until this point during the last "single" fifteen years, I had never even been successful in bringing love to myself. The difference this time was that none of the usual and customary criteria I had used to make prior decisions were there. Now both my brains and my loins remained mute, and all the bells and whistles that accompanied this attraction were spiritually instigated.

Again, Terry and I sent flowers and again I wrote, "You're wonderful," only this time I understood the true meaning. Fourteen years earlier, well into my separation from Jack, I was sitting on a plane waiting for it to begin to taxi. A thick melancholia began to wash over me. At this point in my life I was drowning in the stuff. Whether it was the mood I was in or the subtle lack of oxygen on the plane, I very quickly nodded off.

When I awoke, I wasn't the same person. I was actually unbelievably happy. I knew the guidance realm had visited me, but what they had come to tell me was completely erased from my memory. You'll be told something important that will affirmatively alter your mood, but you won't be allowed to remember why, at least not at the time, because you're meant to live it out in the physical realm to consecrate your life. I think of this as the dangling carrot of the spiritual world. All I could cull from their visit was one sentence, which I would desperately cling to: "You will have a wonderful life!"

And only when I stood in the floral shop writing "You're wonderful" on a card for the second time to this man that I hardly knew did I suddenly see and understand the connection my guidance realm had laid out for me fourteen years ago. Was Jerry about to be "my wonderful life"? A tear rolled down my cheek.

When the guidance realm hands you your marching orders, it's best to simply follow them without question. The important thing is to trust first—understanding can arrive later.

But there are things in this world that we can avoid but can't deny, and my sudden surge of emotions for Jerry were as obvious as, well, a startling shock of electrical charge.

I am, by nature, an impatient person, living by the motto

"Don't put off 'til today what you could have done yesterday." I feel the same way about others, and after tapping my foot and waiting from August to November to hear from Jerry, I decided to put the "personal" part of the equation on hold to pursue our original business directive. I asked Ronnie Meyer if he knew Jerry, although I could easily guess at the answer, since Ronnie knew everybody. I requested that he call him to see if he was interested in adding his name to the board of directors of Moonview. Ronnie made the call, and the next day he filled me in on the conversation—what little there was of it.

"I'm not sure I did a good job," Ronnie told me. He had a tough time getting those words out, perhaps because they were new to him. Ronnie always did a good job. He felt especially bad, having the sense that he had failed me. Jerry had been as evasive as a butterfly in spring, finally saying that he didn't know if there was a business in Moonview. Ronnie replied with a tart, "It's the business of saving souls." But at that juncture the only soul Jerry was interested in was his own.

My reaction was to get angry, quietly perhaps, but still mad. I don't mind being turned down; I just assume that if you're bothered by failure, then life isn't the business for you. But what I do mind greatly is being placed neatly on a shelf and forgotten. But I was in no position to blame anyone else for forgetting, as I then remembered that I had never given Jerry our five-year projection to even put on a shelf.

It was at this time that my ex-husband, Jack, his mother, Magda, our son, Aaron, my occasional boyfriend, Steve, and I were all taking my daughter, Jesse, to Atlantic City for her twenty-first birthday. (Every Jewish mother should teach her daughter how to drink and gamble. After all, our religion is all about overcoming hardships.) Our little caravan decided to stop off in New York first. Picking up the phone, I called Jerry to ask for an impromptu meeting. We agreed to meet for dinner and have a conference call with Peter Ratican, the consulting chief financial officer of Moonview.

I put on my classiest business suit, and neatly tucked our five-year projection plan and a nondisclosure agreement into my briefcase. I made a point of looking as professional as possible. I didn't want him to see me as just that woman who couldn't leave a room without hugging.

Having been lucky enough to travel the globe, I don't believe there's a more romantic spot on earth than Manhattan at night. There's excitement pulsating all around you, but it doesn't infringe on the perfect bubble in which two people can lock themselves. The city becomes a carnival backdrop for lovers to glide through while holding hands.

My first evening alone with Jerry was nothing like that. I don't know what I expected when we sat down at our table in the restaurant. Our relationship thus far had been professionally cordial, and I had to assume that he thought the hugs and the flowers were just something that people who live in Hollywood do, the way Eskimos rub noses.

Here was a man who was legendary in the business world for laying out the facts in front of him, weighing them, and then

carving his decision in cement. I already knew from the conversation he'd had with Ronnie which way he was leaning, and
my objective for the evening was to lay out all of my hopes for
Moonview in business terms I thought he would understand. I
felt like I was back in high school cramming for a test. It was
instantly apparent that I needn't have bothered. Although we
connected even before we draped the linen napkins on our laps,
it was on a spiritual level. As I quickly discovered, that was
where Jerry needed warmth and understanding the most.

His opening salvo, not exactly a line I had ever had the gift
of being asked, was "I'm wondering if you could share with me
your spiritual belief system about death." In all my forty-nine
years, it was truly the first time a man had asked me to share my
purpose and my way. I asked Jerry to tell me what he believed
his purpose was. He pondered the question and replied, "I want
to make an impact."

As the minutes passed, the room disappeared. The waiter's
attendance became an unwelcome intrusion. The pull between
us was obvious, fused by an intensity that blurred my every
visual other than his face. Space and time evaporated, and we
lost ourselves in each other's eyes, as though we were somehow
being reunited. It was as though our hearts knew a secret they
wouldn't tell us. The dinner became a philosophic reflection of
our lonely interiors.

Jerry told me that when he was growing up his mother had
wanted him to be a rabbi, but with the push and pull that often
goes on between parents and children, he went to college and

studied the New Testament instead. He was taken by and found he had a certain affinity with the teachings of Christ and majored in Bible literature at Haverford College (a Quaker school). As with many of us, his quest to get ahold of his truest and deepest beliefs ended abruptly when he entered the world of business, and between meetings and deals and gastrointestinal reflux, he forged a life stamped by "benign indifference."

The following hours dropped like dominoes as we lingered over coffee and dessert and talked. And talked. I watched as the brick wall that surrounded him slowly began to chip away, and a different man started to emerge. The corporate world has the knifelike ability to sever a personality into two. One is worn like a suit of armor while the other half, the one that houses the best of us, hides quietly inside for fear of showing the world any of our tender weaknesses.

On this night, Jerry began opening doors to his personality that he had closed and bolted years earlier. He told me that he had epilepsy, and then looked surprised that those words flew out of his own mouth: "I've never told anyone. . . ."

"You've never told anyone?" I asked in disbelief.

"Well, only my two wives," he said. My girlfriend's words came stampeding back into my head, "You were married before." In my own mind I tried to sort out if his adding me to that short list carried with it a special implication that even he hadn't stopped to decipher.

Across the table from me was a man who had survived in both business and life by closing himself off and maintaining his own counsel. And yet he felt comfortable enough with me, protected enough with me, to allow his innermost emotions to pour out of him. I felt I had to do the same.

I took Jerry through all my beliefs concerning death, life after life, dreams, and the guidance realm that protects us. Then I stopped. Did I dare tell him that I channeled? I took a gulp and reckoned with what made me *me*. At minimum, if he was going to be a part of Moonview, he was soon to know my life's work anyway.

"I've spoken to Jon," I finally blurted out. One look into Jerry's face, I needed to keep going. "He told me that he chose his death. He knew he could touch more people's lives from the other side than one classroom at a time. Jon chose the brutality of his murder, because the horror of that event blew open your heart."

There was no turning back now, so I continued. "Jon also told me that you're in an unhappy marriage, one that was good for the climb up the corporate ladder, a mental marriage with no intimacy. Jon told me that he has work to do with you. Together, you will touch many lives. Jon stood for inspiration, peace, and healing. And together you will fulfill that mission."

I watched what reaction would come back at me. It wasn't the one I had expected. This man who hardly knew me, who had never shared a meal alone with me before, looked intensely and unwaveringly into my eyes and said, "I believe you."

Leaving the restaurant that night, I handed Jerry my prospectus for Moonview. I gave it to him in the hope that he would get a deeper sense of me, for I had put so much of myself into my dream project that I couldn't help but consider it less of a business plan and more like a diary. But I was worried that in his mind he would reexamine everything I had said and done that evening and think that it was all done for purely business purposes.

Jerry offered to drive me home. (Something, I later found out, he never did.) But a lift was unnecessary, as the hotel where I was staying was just across the street from the restaurant.

With all the papers I'd handed him in his hand, he disappeared into the Manhattan night.

Steve was waiting for me in our room when I returned to the hotel. He asked me how it had gone, although I had learned over the course of our rocky relationship that my answers were of little interest to him. I told Steve it was best to end our relationship. I was always at my most attractive to him whenever I was ending our relationship.

"That man came on to you, didn't he?" Steve asked, afraid of losing what he never really enjoyed having.

"No, no, but that man knew me better in three hours than you've known me in two years," I sadly stated.

He heard that, and with that our on-again, off-again affair was off for the last time.

This was what I would call a "big" night, one filled with signs. I didn't know if Jerry and I would ever have a relationship, but now, after forty-nine years, I was experiencing with certainty the kind of relationship I wanted. I "showed up" and all of me was valued; a man "showed up" who bared his soul.

What I didn't know was that Jerry had gone home only to stay up all night reading the prospectus on Moonview. He read it as a businessman, then he read it like a man who felt he may have just discovered that road not taken he had been searching for.

When I returned to Los Angeles, Jerry and I talked for two days. I don't mean that we talked twice on two separate days. I'm saying that we talked straight through for two solid days, only taking time away from the phone for a quick catnap or to pop a little something into the microwave. There wasn't even the tiniest stone in either of our lives that we left unturned. The joys, hurts, dreams, defeats, successes, and sorrows were all laid out and shared. In that forty-eight-hour burst of time we had come to know each other better and deeper and fuller than we knew anyone else on earth. I trusted this man completely, and I completely loved him.

As this marathon finally came to a close, I was both exhausted and unburdened. I thought we had said everything there was to say. Jerry had one thing more: "I don't want to get divorced," he whispered into the phone.

Indeed, now there was definitely no more to say.

There are times when looking on the bright side requires a high-powered telescope just to find it. The belief system I had been building within myself for years had smacked up against reality, and in those kinds of wrestling matches, reality's the one that usually puts you in a headlock. *But what*, I had to ask myself, *was the reality?* He had made it very clear that any future I envisioned us sharing together was impossible. Still, all that I had learned and felt and believed told me that finally knowing a man like Jerry was, in itself, a harbinger of hope. At least now I knew there were, indeed, men like Jerry out there—men who would be able to understand me, and, with that understanding, love me even more. I was okay.

The next morning I meditated, and again Jon came to me. He said that I should tell his father that I wanted to be his wife. That, I told myself immediately, was impossible. "Are you nuts?" I cried. It was one thing to write, "You're wonderful" to accompany a bouquet, or call at 6:30 in the morning with absolutely nothing to say, but to tell someone you've only really known for two full days that you want to marry him—no way in hell would I do that.

I had done all I could to keep a lid on my desires, repeating to myself Falstaff's line that "the better part of valor is discretion." But quoting Shakespeare can only get you so far, and now, with Jon prodding me on, I knew with unbending certainty that I had finally met the man who really seemed to want to hear the music that my heart beat to—perhaps for the first time in my life.

I had never met Jon when he was alive, but I found that I trusted him as much as anyone I ever knew. Still, I didn't know if what he asked of me was possible. Then my phone rang. It was Jerry. "I have something to tell you," he said.

"I have something to tell you, too," I whispered, steeling my courage for the one moment I realized would define my future.

"You go first," Jerry said.

It was then that my courage quickly ran for cover, and instead of blatantly coming out and saying "I want to marry you," I used the truth of that morning like Styrofoam puffballs packaged around something fragile to protect my ego. "I meditated this morning and Jon came to tell me to tell you that I want to be your wife."

Silence. Followed by more silence.

At last I heard Jerry's voice again, tightened and slowed by tears, "I just called to ask you to marry me." We found ourselves connected in the silent conviction that it was Jon who had orchestrated our unlikely union. I held the phone close to my ear as Jerry began to cry the welcoming tears that a new life and a new relationship with his son were returned to him.

I had spent my life hiding pieces of myself in the shadows, trying desperately to fit in, shaving away aspects of my personality and my beliefs in an attempt to make myself acceptable to my parents, my husband, and my friends. I had dreams of being a messenger of God; in reality, I couldn't even be a true messenger for myself. Only when I trusted in myself and the guidance realm was I able to find someone who loved my truest essence.

Jerry had wanted "to put the poetry back into his life." I now entered his life to love him fully because he could finally feel his own fullness and own his own poetry. Our love is more than either of us could have ever imagined for ourselves. Every morning we vow to see the deep perfection of every moment, to swim beyond the surface where design is Divine, and to inspire the perpetual kiss between heaven and earth.

Postscript

There is one spectacle grander than the sea,
that is the sky; there is one spectacle grander
than the sky, that is the interior of the soul.

VICTOR HUGO

MOONVIEW SANCTUARY OPENED ITS DOORS in September
2004. Those doors are located in Santa Monica, but we keep
the precise address a well-guarded secret.

Part of our mission was to "transcend existing models of
client care through a team of experts who create a constantly
interactive system for growth". That team of ace doctors on
hand at a moment's notice to "think tank" and customize
treatments would be expensive. The model would never be

reimbursable. We knew we would attract clients who could not risk exposure from any paper trail. Although this would not be our mind-set, the clients might feel that their time was money, "give me the best and brightest pit crew to get me on my way quickly." For some their time was a premium, yes, yet they also were aware that our more pervasive results overrode their insurance copay. Some of our clients were from out of the country and insurance simply did not apply.

Politicians had constituents, CEOs had shareholders, sports and entertainment had schedules to protect. The headlights of the press could ignite huge damage cycles. Our vow became to "maintain the highest possible caliber of confidentiality for our participants." Our silent mission was to have these privileged participants help fund a new model of care, then we in turn would give the model to the public.

As anyone who picks up a newspaper knows, Los Angeles is a breeding ground for the paparazzi, and there's nothing more luscious to their lens than a celebrity teetering on the abyss. We consider it our responsibility to shield our patients' lives as well as their reputations when they finally make the decision to seek the help and transformation they've long needed. We insist they be able to maintain their privacy, even from other patients. (We're careful that they never accidentally "bump" into each other, so the staff is vigilant in synchronizing times and location so that each patient feels that Moonview is theirs exclusively for the length of their stay.)

Certainly many of those who seek out Moonview have

similar, high-powered lives, making for similar psychological and physical problems. But each of those individuals remains unique, and only after getting to know them and their families does the medical staff create and design the best program for them to follow. We don't believe in or subscribe to the idea of "one size fits all." Hat salesmen know that not every head is shaped the same; neither are the needs, desires, anxieties, or depressions that swirl underneath that hat. Combining both Eastern and Western healing sciences, it's our goal not only to help the client through a current crisis but to supply tools that they can use for the rest of their lives. (Maybe it's the mother in me, but our hope is that no one leaves Moonview without a solid tether of support, constantly monitored for a year by our staff. If a client wants less, that's alright, too.)

Does Moonview resemble the vision I had originally conceived those many years ago? I honestly don't know. Back then it was a dream, and dreams are really hopes flying on the magic carpet of imagination. To turn Moonview into a reality, we assembled the best possible team of therapists, psychiatrists, and doctors to board the boat for this new venture. Now it's their dream as well. But, yes, the heart and soul of Moonview remains true to the original spark that ignited it.

What I didn't anticipate was that Jerry would become our template for all the patients and their families who come through the door. Like all those who come to the Sanctuary, Jerry was and remains an overachiever. But now the goals he sets for himself are for his own pleasure and fulfillment.

Personally, I like overachievers. I've worked with them, I've lived with them, I've loved them, and, yes, I have to admit, I am one of them. Overachievers always have one personality trait in common: They accomplish more than onlookers expect of them, but always a little less than they expect from themselves. This can turn even the grandest success into a heartbreaking failure.

Robert Browning, who's always good for a quote, said "Ah, but a man's reach should exceed his grasp, or what's a heaven for?" I don't wish to get into an argument with Mr. Browning, but it's that kind of philosophy that causes depression, burnout, and slipped discs.

That said, of course, the great poet is right. The trouble is, when we concentrate all of our overachieving into one specific area, the other regions of our lives, like family and spirituality, go unattended. (The Brownings had a wonderful, caring marriage, proving that he was wise enough to grasp high for all of the truly important things that fill a life.) Jerry had grasped high, his achievements swelled, and in his climb managed to lose everything that could have comforted him in his tumble from corporate grace. At sixty-three he had to start from scratch, learning about love, spirituality, and his real place in the world. I'm just happy he's decided that his real place is beside me.

When we're not at Moonview, Jerry and I are crisscrossing the country visiting our seven grandchildren. I could say how many are his and how many are mine, but our hearts refuse to divvy them up that way. When I glance back at my life and then look at all the love that surrounds me now, I realize those movies my mother took me to as a child were true; a happy ending is really just a happy beginning. As Elizabeth Bowen said, "When you love someone, all your saved-up wishes start coming out."

NOTE TO THE READER

AND HERE, DEAR READER, IS THE WALTZ I would like to do with you. I put out a call for my partners, the angels, and God to now come forward once again. May they join me in this prayer for you: "Be gentle with yourselves. Love each and every piece of your existence. Wonder in every moment how you are *love*. See the beauty and magnificence in everything you do and everyone you touch. You are one with God. You are the master of your own fate. Wisely chart the course of your soul. Rest easy that you are not alone and that those around you are truly in service to your well-being. Love your life. Love all dimensions of your life. See yourself in the *all*. God bless your soul. We are *all one*."

ABOUT THE
AUTHOR

DR. LAURIE ANN LEVIN,
former talent agent and Hollywood producer, now a clinical psychologist, is founder
and CEO of Moonview Sanc-
tuary, a psychiatric and transformational institute in Santa Monica, California (www.moonviewsanctuary.com).

Through the collaborative integration of medicine, psychology and neuroscience, along with ancient wisdom and
holistic healing arts, Moonview Sanctuary is unique in the field
of mental health. Sixty-five practioners come together from
diverse cultures to share their knowledge and inspire new
methodologies for the customized care of each patient.

Dr. Levin also created a new form of psychoanalysis, Soul
Communion™, as well as a patent pending for self-transfor-
mation and starting a collective endeavor. Framing her practice
on the foundation of life after life, Dr. Levin focuses on helping people use Soul Communion™ to explore new frontiers of
health and spirituality. Continue your own exploration by visiting her website (www.laurieannlevin.com).

Family portrait, 1953.

Mr. and Mrs. Stanley and
Germaine Perlman,
October 18, 1946.

Family portrait,
Jesse, age 1, Jack and me.

Divorced but happy,
Aaron's nursery school
graduation.

Mom and Dad visit,
Pacific Palisades, CA
1989.

Jesse's NYU
graduation, 2005.

Aaron's NYU graduation, 2006,
with Grandma Magda.

My doctoral graduation from Ryokan College, 1999.

Jerry and me, Miami Beach, January 1, 2005, two days after our wedding.

Jonathan Levin
Our watchful guardian angel whose wingspan includes us all.